# Covenant Motherhood

# *Covenant Motherhood*

## REFLECTING THE ROLE OF CHRIST IN OUR LIVES

STEPHANIE DIBB SORENSEN

Covenant Communications, Inc.

Cover image: *A Widow's Mite* copyright © by Annie Henrie. Courtesy of Altus Fine Art. For print information, visit www.altusfineart.com.

Author photo courtesy of Noelle DeGroot Photography

Cover design copyright © 2013 by Covenant Communications, Inc.

Published by Covenant Communications, Inc.
American Fork, Utah

Copyright © 2013 by Stephanie Dibb Sorensen
All rights reserved. No part of this book may be reproduced in any format or in any medium without the written permission of the publisher, Covenant Communications, Inc., P.O. Box 416, American Fork, UT 84003. This work is not an official publication of The Church of Jesus Christ of Latter-day Saints. The views expressed within this work are the sole responsibility of the author and do not necessarily reflect the position of The Church of Jesus Christ of Latter-day Saints, Covenant Communications, Inc., or any other entity.

General Authority quotes copyright © 2013 by IRI, Inc.

Printed in the United States of America
First Printing: March 2013

19 18 17 16 15 14 13      10 9 8 7 6 5 4 3 2 1

ISBN-13: 978-1-62108-317-7

For Grant, Clark, and Natalie, who gave me both the title of "Mother" and all the tutoring that comes with it. And for Matt, because he let me be the mother of his children and lovingly endures the disparity between what I know and what I do.

# Acknowledgments

HALF OF THE CREDIT FOR this book goes to my husband. When I felt the continued prompting to write but couldn't figure out how to possibly make it work, Matt said, "Make a schedule, and I'll help with the kids. Just do it." And he did help and offer encouragement throughout the whole process. I'm also thankful to Becca Wilhite, Katie Child, and Samantha Millburn for helping a rookie navigate the world of publishing. They miraculously made me feel up to the task. Conversations with my friend Shantel Gardner became the foundation of this book as we delved into the doctrine of motherhood, and I still love her insights and friendship. Thank you to all the friends who helped me talk through the principles and details of *Covenant Motherhood* at lunch, over the phone, or via e-mail. Finally, it would be silly to write a book about the influence of mothering without recognizing my finest example—my own mother. Thank you, Mom, for being the kind of person who gave me confidence and faith to tackle the hardest job in the world. You show me how to love motherhood, and you're always there for me on the bad days too.

# Contents

Acknowledgments . . . . . . . . . . . . . . . . . . . . . . . . . . . . . . . . . . . vii

Introduction: Motherhood Testifies of Christ . . . . . . . . . . . . . . . . . . 1

Chapter 1: Jesus Christ Creates . . . . . . . . . . . . . . . . . . . . . . . . . . . 7

Chapter 2: Jesus Christ Teaches . . . . . . . . . . . . . . . . . . . . . . . . . 13

Chapter 3: Jesus Christ Succors . . . . . . . . . . . . . . . . . . . . . . . . . 21

Chapter 4: Jesus Christ Provides . . . . . . . . . . . . . . . . . . . . . . . . . 27

Chapter 5: Jesus Christ Cleanses . . . . . . . . . . . . . . . . . . . . . . . . 35

Chapter 6: Jesus Christ Defends and Protects . . . . . . . . . . . . . . . . 43

Chapter 7: Jesus Christ Loves and Sacrifices . . . . . . . . . . . . . . . . . 51

Chapter 8: Jesus Christ Forgives and Shares Burdens . . . . . . . . . . . 59

Chapter 9: Jesus Christ Saves . . . . . . . . . . . . . . . . . . . . . . . . . . 69

Chapter 10: Grace and the Covenant . . . . . . . . . . . . . . . . . . . . . . 79

Chapter 11: The Eternal Influence of Covenant Motherhood . . . . . . 87

# Introduction:
## *Motherhood Testifies of Christ*

I REMEMBER ONE EARLY MORNING when I was awakened by my three-year-old, Clark. He pulled apart my eyelids with his chubby little fingers and shined a flashlight directly into my eyeball. "Wake up, Mommy, wake up!"

This particular morning came toward the end of what seemed like the longest recorded winter in history. My husband and I were in the middle of the challenging young-family stage of life. He worked full time during the day, went to law school in the evening, and studied late into the night. I was the primary caregiver for our three small children, ages four, three, and one. Their care demanded all of my time and energy, and I often felt overwhelmed. On that morning, I was far too exhausted for the day to begin with a flashlight, and my reaction was not reverent because it woke up one-year-old Natalie.

Moments like this were stark reminders of my motherhood reality: sleep had become the new currency by which I measured my day and my sanity, and with Clark's harsh awakening and a crying baby, I was already starting in a deficit. One of my supposedly potty-trained boys had a messy accident to deal with, and when I staggered from my bedroom down the hall into the kitchen, I found an open tub of yogurt smeared across the kitchen floor. They don't put this stuff in those *What to Expect* books because they know the world population would be threatened.

I stepped across the yogurt, looked out the window, and saw almost a full foot of new snow on the deck. If I'd had the energy, I would have fallen into a heap on the floor. With my left retina still burning, I began to fantasize about running away to an exotic beachfront location and sleeping in a large, luxurious hotel bed. By myself. Nevertheless, the day called. I took a deep breath, grumbled to myself, and reached for the paper towels . . . and probably a handful of chocolate chips.

Such episodes of fatigue and burnout are common in the realm of motherhood, but the daily details actually embody powerful symbols of Jesus Christ's mission and our covenant relationship with Him. Motherhood is deep, wide, and relentless, and occasionally, it drags us to our limits. These are the moments when it can be a challenge to have a glowing testimony of what we have been taught about motherhood: "Motherhood is near to divinity. It is the highest, holiest service to be assumed by mankind. It places her who honors its holy calling and service next to the angels."[1]

The sleep-deprived, stretch-marked, unshowered side of us may react with a nuance of bitterness to such a claim. And yet, deep down inside of us, there is something that knows it is true: Motherhood is divine. It is a calling. While I have never lost faith in the eternal importance of motherhood, I have sometimes struggled to find meaning in the daily, seemingly mundane tasks of a mother—to recognize the divinity down there in the trenches.

I am less than one decade into my motherhood experience—which, according to a supposedly scientific online study, means I've changed approximately 11,388 diapers—but I am slowly gaining a conviction and understanding of the divine power in this role I have chosen. I thought I understood it before I had children, but then . . . well, then I had children. Among the earliest realizations was how much I still had to learn.

In the moments when our senses are overwhelmed by the details, it can be so helpful to have a clear understanding of our role, our influence, and our commitment. Motherhood is one of the most important opportunities we have to become like Jesus Christ. The service we do for our children, even the simple things, is a symbol of the service Jesus Christ performs for us.

There are certainly many moments of joy in motherhood. Mothers everywhere can testify of the happiness that comes from the smell of a newborn right after a bath or the way her sweet head fits exactly in the space where your neck and collarbone meet. There are first steps and first smiles and the first "Mama." You see your son hug and kiss his sibling. You hear a child's sincere prayer of faith. Your shy daughter excels in her gymnastics class and smiles at you with pride. You pick up your nine-year-old son from school, and he still lights up and runs to the van every time you arrive. Your child wins Student of the Week. Your daughter is the only one of her friends who wears a modest dress to prom, and she positively glows. A nervous, adolescent voice gives a sacrament meeting talk and bears sweet testimony. One Saturday in your life, your children wake up early and do their chores on their own. Just once though, so you enjoy it while you can. They excel. They learn. They grow. They make you proud.

Loving your children is easy. Enjoying all of the responsibilities that come with actually mothering them is not as easy. Motherhood is a messy symphony of joy and discouragement, satisfaction and guilt, determination and exhaustion, faith and fear. Raising children well stretches all of our feelings and all of our abilities, sometimes in painful ways.

From my first days of motherhood, my soul began stretching in ways I had never anticipated. I wanted to raise up children to the Lord and teach them the doctrines and practices of the gospel of Jesus Christ. I wanted to help them become the whole souls they were meant to become when they left the presence of their Heavenly Father and found their way into my care. Motherhood, however, is a package deal. It certainly includes a large measure of teaching, loving instruction, and example, but it is also fraught with exhausting daily details. In the midst of those tiring tasks, it is easy to lose sight of the powerful doctrine inherent in a mother's role.

President Boyd K. Packer stated, "Virtues and attributes upon which perfection and exaltation depend come naturally to a woman and are refined through marriage and motherhood."[2] Ironically, this refining pathway to exaltation puts us face-to-face with our weaknesses and frailties. As I became a mother and embraced the overwhelming responsibility of raising a child, I discovered new flaws in my character and quickly recognized my dependence upon the Lord. I prayerfully studied the scriptures and pored over the teachings of our living prophets, seers, and revelators, trying to make sense of my new role, the one I was born to do. I listened to testimonies, watched other mothers, and spent a lot of time thinking about what it all meant. I began to understand that even though I am not a perfect mother, my experience as a mother is designed to help me become perfect. Even small acts of service put me in Christ's footsteps. He testified in Moses 6:62–63 (emphasis added): "And now, behold, I say unto you: *This is the plan of salvation unto all men*, through the blood of mine Only Begotten, who shall come in the meridian of time. And behold, *all* things have their likeness, and *all things are created and made to bear record of me*, both things which are temporal, and things which are spiritual; things which are in the heavens above, and things which are on the earth, and things which are in the earth, and things which are under the earth, both above and beneath: *all things bear record of me*."

*Everything* we do to help our children progress is meant to point us to Christ. All of those mundane tasks: folding laundry, doing dishes, making lunches, wiping spills, running errands, finding socks, taking temperatures, making appointments, calling teachers, stopping arguments, changing diapers, and scraping unknown substances off the walls—*all* of these things—are symbols of some part of the Savior's atoning mission. It is no accident that these tasks are continuous. They are repeated over and over to bear record of Him. Elder Neal A. Maxwell stated,

> Repeatedly God has described His course as reiterative, "one eternal round." . . . We mortals sometimes experience boredom in the routine repetition of our mortal tasks, including even good works; and thus vulnerable, we are urged not to grow weary in well doing. . . . But given God's divine love, there is no boredom on His part amid His repetitive work, for his course, though one eternal round, involves continuous redemption for His children; it is full of goodness and mercy as His long-suffering shows His love in action. In fact we cannot even comprehend the infinite blessings which await the faithful—"eye hath not seen, nor ear heard."[3]

In all other areas of our worship, we participate in repetitive rituals. And likewise, as we repeat over and over again acts of kindness, service, and sacrifice, we become more like Jesus Christ and our Heavenly Father. Repetition is key to Heavenly Father's plan. Our Church meetings are structured exactly the same each week. We hear the sacrament prayers repeated word for word and make the same promises week after week. Each time we go to the temple, we participate in ordinances repetitive in nature. We are not discouraged by the sameness of it all; we recognize that these rituals serve a purpose in our Christian development.

This repetition refines our discipleship; however, in motherhood, we tend to become more easily frustrated by the daily, repeated tasks we participate in. Perhaps as we begin to recognize the same powerful symbolism, potential, and influence in our daily lives that we value in our other forms of worship, we can begin to see things "as they really are."[4]

Elder Maxwell also taught on another occasion,

> The divine delight in what seems to us to be mere repetition is one clue to the sublime character of God. Since we must, at times, accept what appears to us to be routine, repeated experiences, we too, if we try, can find fresh meaning and fresh joy in the repeated experiences. God's course is one eternal round but it is not one monotonous round. God is never bored, for one who has perfect

love is never bored. There is always so much to notice, so much to do, so many ways to help, so many possibilities to pursue.⁵

We can discover the "fresh meaning" Elder Maxwell alludes to in a careful study of the ministry and mission of Jesus Christ. Motherhood is a reflection of our covenant relationship with our Savior, and it is a relationship designed to lift us and help us experience joy. It seems to be an unspoken covenant in itself. Any Latter-day Saint mother who loves the Lord desires to raise up children unto Him, and by receiving unto ourselves a spirit child of our Heavenly Father, we, much like Hannah of the Old Testament, promise, "O Lord of hosts, if thou wilt indeed look on the affliction of thine handmaid, and remember me, and not forget thine handmaid, but wilt give unto thine handmaid a . . . child, then I will give him unto the Lord all the days of his life."⁶

Our covenants become key landmarks on our journey to become more like the Savior. As we cling to and focus on our promises to the Lord and His promises to us, we are refined and prepared for our eternal destiny.

The *Gospel Principles* manual defines a covenant as "a sacred agreement or mutual promise between God and a person or a group of people."⁷ Even from our youth, we make such promises, such as when we participate in ordinances like baptism and partaking of the sacrament. In doing so, we enter into a covenant relationship with Heavenly Father and Jesus Christ "in which we are assured salvation from the consequences of sin if we are obedient."⁸ The Savior promises us the possibility of salvation through His Atonement and through our obedience, but that is not all. He also offers us guidance, love, and instruction to help us keep our part of the covenant. As mothers, we emulate the Savior through our service in our own homes and families, and in doing so, we prepare ourselves and our children for His eternal rewards. Sister Julie B. Beck explained,

> Oh, that every girl and woman would have a testimony of her potential for eternal motherhood as she keeps her earthly covenants.
> . . .
> Covenant-keeping women with mother hearts know that whether motherhood comes early or late; whether they are blessed with a "quiver full" of children here in mortality or not; whether they are single, married, or left to carry the responsibility of parenthood alone—in holy temples they are "endowed with power from on high" (D&C 38:32), and with that endowment they received the promised

blessings and are "persuaded of them, and embraced them" (Heb. 11:13).

Every girl and woman who makes and keeps sacred covenants can have a mother heart.[9]

Covenants are the keys by which we access eternal blessings. Sister Susan W. Tanner said that "serving families is a way of covenant keeping, and covenant keeping reaps the promised blessing of having the Spirit in our lives."[10] When we mother with the Holy Ghost as our companion, our eyes can be opened, and we can see the powerful symbolism, potential, and influence of our role—even among the dreary details—and we can recognize how motherhood binds us to Jesus Christ. President Ezra Taft Benson taught, "That [wo]man is greatest and most blessed and joyful whose life most closely approaches the pattern of the Christ. This has nothing to do with earthly wealth, power, or prestige. The only true test of greatness, blessedness, joyfulness is how close a life can come to being like the Master, Jesus Christ. He is the right way, the full truth, and the abundant life."[11]

This book will explore how the mission, message, and ministry of Jesus Christ are reflected in our continuous mothering. Each chapter will analyze the various roles of Jesus Christ in His mission, how our roles as mothers emulate and reflect those of the Savior, and how we can contribute to furthering His mission. As we recognize the symbols of our covenant relationship with Him in all that we do, we can draw closer to Him and begin to find more meaning and joy in His service.

CHAPTER 1

## Jesus Christ Creates

OUR SAVIOR'S MISSION IS so broad and far-reaching, and yet it is focused and personal. Though it's sometimes hard to recognize, we participate in making His amazing work more intimate as we fulfill our eternal role as mothers. One of His principal roles and titles is *Creator*. From the tiny, complex, subatomic particles to the vast wonder of oceans and skies, He literally created "worlds without number"[1] at His Father's side. Together They created man and woman, God's own glorious offspring. They made it all and saw "that it was very good."[2]

In a divine dose of the miraculous, God lets us collaborate with Him in the full scope of creation, even in creating life itself. From the moment of conception to the poignant occasion of childbirth, our bodies act as vessels for the genesis and nurture of new life. In an unfolding marvel beyond human comprehension and in an act literally teeming with divine fingerprints, our mother-bodies build cells and nerves and organs and systems and flesh and blood. They enable the creation of a life, a beautiful new being—a new body to house the soul of God's very own child. Elder M. Russell Ballard marveled, "Can anyone witness the miracle of birth and not feel a divine, providential influence? Can anyone look into the face of a precious newborn child and not see etched in its tiny lines and creases the confluence of eternity with mortality?"[3]

Whether we actually give birth to children in our lifetime or not, Heavenly Father has designed all of His daughters as cocreators. Our creative nature is in the very blueprint of our physical bodies, and it is part of our eternal identity. Sister Sheri Dew pointed out that Eve was called "the mother of all living" before she had any children because the title of mother reflected her divine role and eternal nature.[4]

God Himself declared that mankind was made in His very image[5] and that the eternal journey of mankind was His work and His glory.[6] It is no accident that our children carry our features. They may have our eyes or smile or distinctive pinky toe. They too are made in *our* image and are patterned after a long line of children who looked like their parents before them. Our offspring are an extension of us, just as we are an extension of our Heavenly Parents. Our children's progression becomes a joint effort with our Heavenly Father; we share in His work, and He shares His glory. This is part of our practice in becoming Godlike parents.

President David O. McKay said, "Let us also teach girls that motherhood is divine, for when we touch the creative part of life, we enter into the realm of divinity."[7] I had always thought that the concept of creation in womanhood was intrinsically tied to a uterus and reproduction and all of the other wonders of baby-making. And it is, but that is not the only way in which we are creators. During a general Relief Society broadcast in 2008, President Dieter F. Uchtdorf taught that creation "is your opportunity in this life and your destiny in the life to come."[8] I began to realize that motherhood—*all* of motherhood, not just the childbirth part—is simply creation in slow motion. We are literally shaping souls like a potter shapes clay, building children and instilling inside of them all of the knowledge, skills, testimony, and power they will need to make successful choices.

Elder Richard G. Scott explained it like this: "As a mother guided by the Lord, you weave a fabric of character in your children from threads of truth through careful instruction and worthy example. . . . It is your sacred right and privilege."[9] There are many analogies that have been used to describe our Heavenly Father's relationship with His children and how He helps us reach our potential: a potter, a silversmith, a weaver, a sculptor, a painter, a gardener—all of these metaphors testify to the creative nature of parenthood and are reflected in our own mothering.

Constant mothering, in slow motion, may appear ordinary. But we don't realize how truly powerful it is. Without appropriate eternal perspective, this slow-motion process can sometimes feel discouraging. President Spencer W. Kimball acknowledged, "Much is said about the drudgery and the confinement of the woman's role in the home. In the perspective of the gospel it is not so. There is divinity in each new life. There is challenge in creating the environment in which a child can grow and develop. There is partnership between the man and woman in building a family which can last throughout the eternities."[10]

He also pointed out how sharing in the creative process with Heavenly Father is a consecrated responsibility: "Mothers have a sacred role. They are partners with God, as well as with their own husbands, first in giving birth to the Lord's spirit children and then in rearing those children so they will serve the Lord and keep his commandments. Could there be a more sacred trust than to be a trustee for honorable, well-born, well-developed children?"[11]

We know Heavenly Father and Jesus Christ created a world where God's children could grow. As part of this divine and creative partnership, mothers also create a world where *their* children live and grow. This mother-made world consists of home and family. We have the opportunity to create homes that are sacred, safe, and sanctified like the temple. Can you think of anything more divine than that? A mother is the temple matron in her own home, doing all she can to make it a place filled with the Spirit of God. A home is a temple because important eternal work takes place there. The mother of the home plays a significant role in creating that environment and in directing the work within.

When I was expecting my first child, I understood that my world would change. I bought tiny socks and diapers. I purchased a crib, a car seat, and other baby necessities. I cleaned and organized the house, making room for the new arrival in our home and in our routines. Despite no previous notable artistic achievement, I found myself painting a mural on the nursery wall to welcome this small baby. My mother-in-law helped me sew curtains and bedding. I reupholstered a rocking chair I'd purchased at a garage sale. I arranged and rearranged the furniture until everything seemed just right.

I think most mothers, biological or not, can relate to the "nesting" phase we go through as we prepare for the arrival of a new child. Even the Savior Himself had a preparation period before He created mankind. In Job 38:4, Christ testified that He "laid the foundations of the earth." There was significant preparation involved in making a world for God's children, and mothers do the same thing. It is just the beginning of our new role as mothers and cocreators with God. We repeat these nesting stages throughout our children's lives. We create routines for back to school, and we do it again for summers. We choreograph family dynamics as our children transition through different levels of maturity and responsibility. And eventually, we set the stage for them to go to college, serve missions, date, marry, and embark on the journey to adulthood.

These creative efforts are not limited to major benchmarks in our children's development; we also tap in to them in our ongoing household management.

When Jesus Christ made the earth by the power of His priesthood, He took matter unorganized and created a world where Heavenly Father's children could live. Even a quick glance at the phrase "matter unorganized" proves that motherhood and creation have something important in common. Anyone who has seen my children's playroom or passed through my entryway or witnessed my laundry in progress knows that matter unorganized is a significant component of my duties. President Uchtdorf taught, "Creation brings deep satisfaction and fulfillment. We develop ourselves and others when we take unorganized matter into our hands and mold it into something of beauty."[12]

Despite my attempts at upholstery and a mural, I do not consider myself to be very creative. However, there is more to creativity than scrapbooking, home decorating, and sewing our children's clothes. Our misperceptions about creativity can stifle our ability to reap satisfaction from our efforts. Sister Mary Ellen Smoot, former Relief Society general president, reassured sisters everywhere that they are more powerful and creative than they realize: "You are creators. Have you ever coaxed a smile from a baby? Have you ever taught someone to forgive? Have you helped someone learn to read? Prepared a family home evening? Organized a family reunion? Possibly you were prompted to do something for a person you go visiting teaching or home teaching to that made a great difference in their lives. If you have done some of these things, you have been creative."[13]

When we recognize that our creative acts mirror the Savior's creative nature, we can begin to appreciate their purpose. As we create, we become more like Jesus Christ. We can find joy in the opportunity to do His work. Loving the Savior leads to loving His work. Sister Smoot continued, "Creation isn't drudgery. Creation flows from love. When we do what we love, we rejoice along the way. If you are unhappy, if you are feeling weary, troubled, or disillusioned, may I ask you to try something? Instead of dwelling on your troubles, focus instead on creating something remarkable, something of eternal significance."[14]

I remember a time during those young-family-with-husband-in-law-school years when I struggled with weariness. I did not feel like I was accomplishing everything I should be doing. I was trying hard to be good and to do what I knew was right. Intellectually, I knew that my efforts as a mother mattered, but I lacked satisfaction. I prayed for a solution to my beleaguered attitude. I studied the gospel and talked to trusted friends. I attended a women's conference specifically seeking an answer, and after my very first workshop, I knew God had answered my prayer.

A young, busy mother spoke about the many typical challenges women face and mentioned that she prayed to love what the Lord loves. That phrase jumped out at me and lingered in my mind, accompanied by the sensation from the Holy Ghost that it was meant for me. *Pray to love what the Lord loves.* It was a breakthrough. As we love and do the work that He does, not only will we find satisfaction, but we will also find joy. That simple request has become a frequent ingredient in my prayers: "Help me, Heavenly Father, to love the things You love. Help me understand Your work and find joy in it."

Answers came slowly as I began to learn about the Savior's different roles and recognize how my work as a mother emulated those roles. I now better understand that within the realm of my own gifts and talents and even within the limitations of my own circumstances, there are many things I can do to create moments of eternal significance.

We learn as we create. We grow in our understanding of our divine nature and our connection to Heavenly Parents. This knowledge, like all gospel knowledge, is something we can take with us for eternity. Elder David A. Bednar taught, "The Father and the Son have entrusted us with a portion of Their creative power and provided specific guidelines for the proper use of that sacred ability to create life and establish an eternal family. How we feel about and use that sacred power in this life will determine in large measure whether additional creative power will be ours in the life to come."[15] Creation is the Savior's work, and it is *our* opportunity. One creative act after another, we establish a home, organize a family, and forge testimonies and futures. From the miracle of childbirth to the miracle of a successful family home evening, we emulate Jesus Christ when we create, and thus we carry out His mission in our daily mothering.

## Chapter 2
## Jesus Christ Teaches

JESUS CHRIST CAME TO EARTH to be our Savior, but He also came to teach us about His Father, His mission, and how we can gain our salvation. He was a teacher in word and in deed. His teachings help us know and love and serve our Heavenly Father. When mothers teach their children about Jesus Christ, they help them come to know and love and serve Him and Heavenly Father. This is one of our most essential responsibilities as mothers in Zion. Elder Neil L. Andersen gave the following testimony and counsel:

> We hold in our arms the rising generation. They come to this earth with important responsibilities and great spiritual capacities. We cannot be casual in how we prepare them. Our challenge as parents and teachers is not to create a spiritual core in their souls but rather to fan the flame of their spiritual core already aglow with the fire of their premortal faith. . . . The stories of Jesus shared over and over bring faith in the Lord Jesus Christ and strength to the foundation of testimony. Can you think of a more valuable gift for our children?
>
> Are the life and teachings of Jesus Christ embedded in the minds and souls of our children? Do they think about the Savior's life when they wonder what to do in their own lives? This will be more and more important in the years ahead.[1]

According to "The Family: A Proclamation to the World," the charge to teach our children is more than a suggestion; it is an obligation. "Parents have a sacred duty to . . . teach [children] to love and serve one another, observe the commandments of God, and be law-abiding citizens wherever they live. Husbands and wives—mothers and fathers—will be held accountable before God for the discharge of these obligations."[2]

Teaching is not easy. Mother days are often busy and noisy and demanding. Sometimes we don't even know we are teaching. One thing mothers can learn from the example of Jesus Christ is that He did not shy away from opportunities to teach; He recognized teaching moments and opened His mouth. In Matthew 4:25–5:2, we read that "there followed him great multitudes of people from Galilee," and He sat down on a mountain and "opened his mouth, and taught them." We now know that great sermon as the Sermon on the Mount. What young mother has not felt the pull of "multitudes" who follow her? Young children are often underfoot and in our shadow. When we stop, sit, and teach, we are doing what the Savior did.

Even Jesus Christ was weary at times. After He learned about the death of His beloved cousin, John the Baptist, Jesus sought solitude. "When Jesus heard of it, He departed thence by ship into a desert place apart." A mother of small children can understand that solitude is often hard to find. The people still "followed him on foot out of the cities." Jesus "saw [the] great multitude, and was moved with compassion toward them," and He taught them and healed them. After awhile, His disciples tried to turn the crowd away, but Jesus said, "They need not depart."[3] When we make the same concessions with our own children, despite our weariness, the Savior will sustain us and send the Holy Ghost to consecrate our teachings for their good and for our strength.

Elder Andersen assured parents that "as you reverently speak about the Savior—in the car, on the bus, at the dinner table, as you kneel in prayer, during scripture study, or in late-night conversations—the Spirit of the Lord will accompany your words."[4] I remember hearing Sister Julie B. Beck speak at a women's conference about intentional parenting and seeking opportunities to teach. It completely changed the way I approached parenting because she taught me to have a purpose and a goal in all of my efforts in my family. She shared the following experience from her personal mothering history:

> Years ago when we were driving our children back and forth to piano lessons, someone said, "Don't you get tired of driving your children to piano lessons?" I said, "Are you kidding? What a great opportunity I have. My children are captive in my car. I have them and we can talk, teach, and ask questions." That was a wonderful opportunity that allowed us to discuss true principles. . . . Do your best to create formal and informal opportunities to teach and help your children.[5]

## Covenant Motherhood

Jesus Christ taught in the temple, in synagogues, in cities, in homes, in crowds, along roads, at feasts and dinner tables, and in desert places (quiet and remote locations). Mothers often find themselves in many of these same locations with children in tow. We are blessed, therefore, with many opportunities to teach and to testify. Our homes, especially, should be places of gospel instruction.

In 1999, the First Presidency issued a letter, calling all parents "to devote their best efforts to the teaching and rearing of their children in gospel principles which will keep them close to the Church." In the same letter, they declared that "the home is the basis of a righteous life, and no other instrumentality can take its place or fulfill its essential functions in carrying forward this God-given responsibility." The First Presidency also counseled families "to give highest priority to family prayer, family home evening, gospel study and instruction, and wholesome family activities. However worthy and appropriate other demands or activities may be, they must not be permitted to displace the divinely-appointed duties that only parents and families can adequately perform."[6]

I remember one occasion when my husband and I struggled to teach a family home evening lesson to our young and rambunctious children. Our kids had had a little bit of a sass problem that particular day, and at one point, my son Clark had even taken a swing at me. This was, of course, completely unacceptable. So when Matt got home from work, I was exhausted, and he was exhausted. We both lay down on our bed, bemoaning our exhausted states. Matt suggested we have a "lying down" family home evening, and I knew right from the start it wasn't going to go well, but I was too lazy to get up and do anything different.

We called all of the kids into our room, basically to gather around our corpses and be instructed. They made paper-bag puppets of themselves and then Matt said we were going to talk about respect and responsibility. After several pathetic attempts to get them to define those terms, we tried to think of examples of respect from the scriptures. Clark volunteered that when Nehor killed Gideon, that wasn't very respectful. This led to a long list of people beating, killing, and destroying one another, with the side note that "that wasn't respectful." I lay there (yes, lay there) rolling my eyes.

Then Matt directed a puppet show that reenacted the way Clark had treated me earlier in the day when I'd told him he couldn't have a playdate with his friend. Unfortunately, the children thought that the representation of their previous poor behavior was hilarious. They couldn't wait until it was their turn to be the puppet and yell at and hit their mother. So our family home evening turned into an unfettered, all-out paper-bag-puppet brawl of people screaming at and beating each other until the puppets lay in tattered shreds on the ground.

Matt wearily tried to make some summary statement about how it's important to be respectful, and then we released our feral children to go play something else. We stood in the kitchen a few minutes later and looked at each other with dumbfounded disbelief. "That was such a bad family home evening," Matt said. We tried to laugh, but we were too tired.

Elder David A. Bednar has taught:

> Each family prayer, each episode of family scripture study, and each family home evening is a brushstroke on the canvas of our souls. No one event may appear to be very impressive or memorable. But . . . our consistency in doing seemingly small things can lead to significant spiritual results. "Wherefore, be not weary in well-doing, for ye are laying the foundation of a great work. And out of small things proceedeth that which is great."[7] Consistency is a key principle as we lay the foundation of a great work in our individual lives and as we become more diligent and concerned in our own homes.[8]

I'm convinced that Elder Bednar is right. Our family home evening was not impressive. Very few of them are. I honestly hope it was *not* memorable to my children. But we did our meager best, and I trust that God somehow made it "count." In the years since, I have seen the patterns of family home evening and family scripture study grow into habits and routines. They are part of the definition of what our family is and does. My children look forward to Monday nights, and they enjoy their assignments and participation. Family gospel study in its many forms rarely turns out how I imagined it, but it always blesses my family.

One instance where we found evidence that our gospel teaching had made a difference was when my oldest son, Grant, was almost eight years old and my husband and I chose to teach him more completely about human intimacy than we had done up to that point. We built upon previous conversations and bore testimony of related gospel principles. A short time later, I had an opportunity between carpools to spend some one-on-one time with Grant. We went to a café and talked while we ate treats. He brought up our discussion about intimacy and asked a few questions, which I answered the best I could.

On the way to our next carpool pick up, Grant sat in the back row of the van, and I noticed he was deep in thought. After awhile, he spoke up and asked another question. I answered the question and then explained that he would probably have friends and other people tell him the direct opposite of what I had just said. I bore my testimony that the Lord's way was the right way even if other people did not agree. He thought again for a minute and then said innocently, "I know someone who sexed before marriage." I was a little nervous about what he might say next, but I asked anyway. "Who?" He sat up straight and said smartly, "Corianton."[9] I felt a flood of gratitude and surprise come over me.

He had actually been paying attention when we taught. He had been listening when we did family scripture study. He'd put the pieces together from our teachings and from the scriptures, and he *got it.* I assured him that he was right, and I'm sure the Holy Ghost did too. It was a testimony to me that our efforts to teach our children really work. That evidence does not come as often as I would like. Our feeble efforts to teach may seem to go largely unnoticed and unheeded, but many scriptures and prophets and apostles bear witness of the potential for lasting influence.

In the Book of Mormon, Enos related that the memory of his father's repeated teachings drove him to pray sincerely and become more fully converted. During a moment of darkness and despair, Alma the Younger remembered his father's words, and they gave him the courage to call out to the Savior. The young stripling warriors remembered their mothers' faith and testimonies and drew upon them for strength. Elder Neil L. Andersen reassures us that "if a child is not listening, don't despair. Time and truth are on your side. At the right moment, your words will return as if from heaven itself. Your testimony will never leave your children."[10]

What should we teach? In Elder Andersen's general conference talk entitled "Tell Me the Stories of Jesus," he admonishes, "To fathers and mothers, to grandfathers and grandmothers, and to those without children of their own who lovingly nurture children and youth, my counsel is to speak more frequently about Jesus Christ. In His holy name is great spiritual power."[11] Doctrine and Covenants 68:25, 28 gives us a specific commandment that parents teach their children "to understand the doctrine of repentance, faith in Christ the Son of the living God, and of baptism and the gift of the Holy Ghost by the laying on of the hands, when eight years old. . . . And they shall also teach their children to pray, and to walk uprightly before the Lord."

Elder Robert D. Hales listed many things that parents should teach to strengthen their children and families. He encouraged us to instruct them how to pray, study the scriptures and the words of living prophets, fast, work, budget time and resources, learn from our ancestors and family history, and recognize and rely upon the Holy Ghost. He added, "Teach our children the significance of baptism and confirmation, receiving the gift of the Holy Ghost, partaking of the sacrament, honoring the priesthood, and making and keeping temple covenants. They need to know the importance of living worthy of a temple recommend and preparing for a temple marriage."[12] Elder M. Russell Ballard added to the list of teaching responsibilities:

> How can [our children] know of these most important matters unless we teach them? According to the scriptures, parents should teach children "that all men, everywhere, must repent, or they can in nowise inherit the kingdom of God" (Moses 6:57). Children should learn "to pray, and to walk uprightly before the Lord" (D&C 68:28), and "to walk in the ways of truth and soberness; . . . to love one another, and to serve one another" (Mosiah 4:15). Our children should know "to what source they may look for a remission of their sins" (2 Ne. 25:26), and they should learn that they are to "love the Lord thy God with all thine heart, and with all thy soul, and with all thy might" (Deut. 6:5).[13]

President Gordon B. Hinckley also pointed out important principles that parents must teach. He warned mothers that our children are in great danger because of Satan's influence. After discussing some of the wicked trends of our day, he said, "I know of no better answer to these foul practices that confront our young people than the teachings of a mother, given in love with an unmistakable warning." One important element of our responsibility to teach is to warn, even from an early age. President Hinckley added, "Teach your children when they are very young and small, and never quit. As long as they are in your home, let them be your primary interest. I take the liberty tonight of suggesting several things that you might teach them. The list is not complete. You can add other items." He continued by exhorting us to teach them to seek for good friends, to value education, to respect their bodies, to avoid illegal drugs *"as they would the plague,"* to be virtuous, and to pray.[14]

These lists are not complete, so we mothers must pray and rely upon the Holy Ghost to help us know what lessons our children need to learn. We must study the scriptures and pore over the teachings of the living prophets so we will be prepared to teach the principles when we are prompted. In

Doctrine and Covenants 11:21, the Lord tells us, "Seek not to declare my word, but first seek to obtain my word, and then shall your tongue be loosed; then, if you desire, you shall have my Spirit and my word, yea, the power of God unto the convincing of [your children]." That is an amazing promise.

The Savior is a perfect example of teaching the right things at the right time. The study of His teachings arms us with the most important lessons our children will need to know. I once did a search throughout the New Testament using the phrase "Jesus said." It was fascinating to see what specific teachings came directly from His mouth, and it helped me focus more on communicating those same principles to my children. I also searched the phrases "Jesus taught," "Jesus answered," "Jesus spoke," and "Jesus testified." I was really interested to discover that out of those four verbs, the action of *answering* was mentioned in the New Testament at least five times more frequently than the other three verbs. That, in itself, teaches an important lesson: the Savior listened to and perceived people's questions and then taught them truth and doctrine through His answers.

This tells me that within regular conversations, I can probably find more opportunities to teach gospel principles by answering or responding to what my children are saying than I can by delivering a lecture or lesson. Another wonderful tool for becoming more like the Savior is to study all of the scriptures listed in the topical guide under the heading "Jesus Christ, Teaching Methods." When we strive to teach as He taught, we develop Christlike attributes and become more like Him. The more we become like the Savior, the more effective we become in our teaching and other mothering duties.

Sister Julie B. Beck delivered a beautiful talk called "Mothers Who Know" to all Relief Society sisters. She testified of the powerful influence our teaching can have: "Mothers who know are always teachers. Since they are not babysitters, they are never off duty. A well-taught friend told me that he did not learn anything at church that he had not already learned at home. His parents used family scripture study, prayer, family home evening, mealtimes, and other gatherings to teach. Think of the power of our future missionary force if mothers considered their homes as a pre–missionary training center. Then the doctrines of the gospel taught in the MTC would be a review and not a revelation. That is influence; that is power."[15] It is important to note that our teaching loses power if it is not accompanied by example and testimony. Elder Jeffrey R. Holland duly warned:

> No child in this Church should be left with uncertainty about his or her parents' devotion to the Lord Jesus Christ. . . .

> I think some parents may not understand that even when they feel secure in their own minds regarding matters of personal testimony, they can nevertheless make that faith too difficult for their children to detect. . . .
>
> Live the gospel as conspicuously as you can. Keep the covenants your children know you have made. Give priesthood blessings. And bear your testimony! Don't just assume your children will somehow get the drift of your beliefs on their own.[16]

I once had the opportunity to attend an Easter conference hosted at Brigham Young University. Seated in front of me was a young couple with two small children who seemed, in my opinion, too young to be attending the event. I was silently annoyed at the parents for bringing along their mildly unruly children. The speakers taught about the Savior's Atonement, and then there was a musical number that focused on Gethsemane. The Spirit was thick in the large auditorium.

When the song was over, there was a quiet moment before the next speaker took the stand, and I heard the mother in front of me whisper to her son, "Do you like it? Do you like the feeling in here?" The young boy whispered back, "I like it because it feels warm and comfortable." My heart softened, and I gained a new respect for that mother. She was a teacher. She was a testifier. She was an example.

John the Baptist's mission, much like ours, was to teach about Jesus Christ. On one occasion, he was testifying of the Savior to two of His followers. He saw Jesus walk past and said, "Behold, the Lamb of God!" I love what happened when John bore his testimony: "And the two disciples heard him speak, and they followed Jesus."[17] This is our goal. Our teachings and our testimonies and our examples will turn our children to the Savior. If they choose to know the Savior, they will love Him, and they will follow Him.

President Spencer W. Kimball promised, "Your Heavenly Father will smile upon you as you live the commandments and teach them to your children. This is the work of the Lord."[18] When we know that we are doing sacred work and that our Heavenly Father honors our efforts, we are prepared to find joy and fulfillment in motherhood. When we teach the gospel and testify, we are fulfilling our covenant relationship with Jesus Christ. We grow closer to Him and become more like He is. Coming to Him through Christlike teaching is one of the many gifts of motherhood.

CHAPTER 3

# Jesus Christ Succors

THE SCRIPTURES GIVE US SO many examples of the Savior's healing hand and influence. My favorite verses about Jesus Christ and the Atonement are in Alma 7:11–12, where Alma explains *what* our Redeemer would feel when He came to earth to partake of the bitter cup of the Atonement and *why* He would suffer those feelings for us: "And he shall go forth, suffering pains and afflictions and temptations of every kind; and this that the word might be fulfilled which saith he will take upon him the pains and the sicknesses of his people. And he will take upon him death, that he may loose the bands of death which bind his people; and he will take upon him their infirmities, that his bowels may be filled with mercy, according to the flesh, *that he may know according to the flesh how to succor his people* according to their infirmities" (emphasis added).

From His suffering was born an infinite ability to succor. Within the details of a mother's days, weeks, months, and years, she also participates in myriad opportunities to succor. Like the Savior does for us, we reach out to our needy children and heal and comfort them the best way we know how, after the pattern of Jesus Christ. He had a gift for taking situations full of contention, pain, and sorrow and replacing them with peace, healing, and comfort. Elder Dallin H. Oaks stated: "Jesus healed many from physical diseases, but He did not withhold healing from those who sought to be 'made whole' from other ailments. Matthew writes that He healed every sickness and every disease among the people (see Matthew 4:23; 9:35). Great multitudes followed Him, and He 'healed them all' (Matthew 12:15). Surely these healings included those whose sicknesses were emotional, mental, or spiritual. He healed them all."[1]

While both we and our children must depend on the Savior for the ultimate healing of physical, emotional, mental, or spiritual suffering, a mother's efforts to heal and comfort her children are a reflection of the Savior's ministry. As we serve, we act in His name, and we become more like He is.

Recently, my daughter woke me up in the middle of the night to tell me she had an accident in her bed. Her sheets were wet, her clothes were wet, and she was cold. I helped her change out of her clothes, washed her body with a warm washcloth, stripped the sheets, started the laundry, and tucked her into a new bed. She asked me to wrap her in the blankets "like a burrito," and I did. I kissed her on the head, she snuggled down into the mattress, smiled, and said good night.

As I walked out of the room, I turned off all the lights, and in the dark journey back to my bed, I was given some thoughts—because sometimes thoughts are *given*, not just *thought*. I reflected on recent news stories of children who were abused or neglected. I thought of people in the world who would have yelled at or beaten their daughter for wetting her bed. I imagined how someone who was caught up in the aftereffects of drug or alcohol use might have ignored her and left her to fend for herself or spend the night in urine-soaked, cold sheets and clothing.

In the middle of all of those heavy thoughts, I felt a keen sense that my Heavenly Father was happy with how I had just treated His little child. I knew He'd noticed it, loved it, and honored it. It felt like I had done exactly what the Savior would have done if He were there. I knew my role as a mother, a woman, and a nurturer was important. But even more than important. It felt divine—God ordained and God beloved—even in all the apparent simplicity of the moment.

Elder Jeffrey R. Holland exhorted us to succor more:

> I ask you to be a healer, be a helper, be someone who joins in the work of Christ in lifting burdens, in making the load lighter, in making things better. As children, when we had a bump or a bruise, didn't we say to Mom or Dad, "Make it better"? Well, lots of people on your right hand and on your left are carrying bumps and bruises that they hope will be healed and made whole. Someone you know is carrying a spiritual or physical or emotional burden of some sort, or some other affliction drawn from life's catalog of a thousand kinds of sorrow. In the spirit of Christ's first invitation to his twelve Apostles, jump into this work. Help people . . . and try to make things better.[2]

How do mothers "make it better"? We fix it the same way the Savior did—with our touch, our reassuring words, our prayers, and our faith.

The New Testament gives account after account of how Jesus' touch made people better. You may remember the story of the woman who had suffered from an issue of blood for many years. She knew that if she could only touch the Savior, she could be healed. And though the curious crowds pressed upon Christ, the woman worked her way closer and closer to Him and reached out and touched the hem of His garment, "for she said within herself, If I may but touch his garment, I shall be whole." She was right. The scriptures tell us that "Jesus turned him about, and when he saw her, he said, Daughter, be of good comfort; thy faith hath made thee whole. And the woman was made whole from that hour."[3]

Like the Savior, our touch heals. When my son Grant was learning to ride a bike, he would often skin his knees on the driveway. He would always run to me so I could kiss it or rub it or bandage it, and then he would return happily to play. When my son Clark rode his sled into the side of the house and suffered a concussion, he found comfort in laying his head on my lap while I stroked his hair. When Natalie got her kindergarten shots and wailed in pain and fear, she hugged me tightly, and I rubbed her back, and then she felt better. Though a mother's touch may not physically heal to the same extent Jesus' does, it *does* give comfort and restore hope and a sense of safety. These are all gifts that originate from Jesus Christ and His love.

Much of this business of succoring is done quietly and privately. When children wake up vomiting in the middle of the night and you rub their back and provide them every comfort within your reach, it is a sacred secret between them and you. It often goes unnoticed even by your husband or other children. That is often how Christ succored. In the book of Matthew, we read the story of a leper who approached Jesus and worshipped him. He asked Jesus to heal him, "and immediately his leprosy was cleansed." As the leper walked away, Jesus requested, "See thou tell no man; but go thy way."[4]

When we nurse the sick and work for their healing, unless we post it on Facebook, our efforts go largely unnoticed. It is the same kind of anonymous service the Savior preferred to give. We may often wish that we received more accolades for our quiet heroics; nevertheless, our secret service helps us practice and emulate the way Jesus ministered and helps grow deep bonds with the children we serve.

Healing and comforting go hand in hand. Where a mother cannot heal, she can still comfort. Like the Savior, who "saw the multitudes, [and] was moved with compassion on them,"[5] we sense when our children are in pain, and we can reach out to them to "make it better." Sister Sheri L. Dew shared an experience from her own childhood that exemplifies a mother's ability to succor: "When I was growing up, it was not uncommon for Mother to wake me in the middle of the night and say, 'Sheri, take your pillow and go downstairs.' I knew what that meant. It meant a tornado was coming, and I was instantly afraid. But then Mother would say, 'Sheri, everything will be OK.' Her words always calmed me. Today, decades later, when life seems overwhelming or frightening, I call Mother and wait for her to say, 'Everything will be OK.'" She then added her testimony of the important role a mother's comfort does and will continue to play in her children's lives:

> We live in a world of uncertainty. Never has there been a greater need for righteous mothers—mothers who bless their children with a sense of safety, security, and confidence about the future, mothers who teach their children where to find peace and truth and that the power of Jesus Christ is always stronger than the power of the adversary. Every time we build the faith or reinforce the nobility of a young woman or man, every time we love or lead anyone even one small step along the path, we are true to our endowment and calling as mothers and in the process we build the kingdom of God.[6]

Jesus Christ could literally calm troubled seas with His faith-filled voice of reassurance. Mothers too hold that power in their homes. Their voices, their words, their gentle touch can restore calm to troubled souls. This motherly influence is lasting. Even as children grow into adults, they remember the gentle reassurances of their mothers. After the terrorist attacks in America on September 11, 2001, First Lady Laura Bush's first instinct was that of a mother: "I called my children immediately as soon as I could get to them, to reassure them," she said, "and then I called my own mother, just for the comfort of her voice."[7]

As our children grow older, the severity of their wounds seems to grow deeper. No longer can a kiss on the knee make everything better. The Savior warned us that we would have tribulation in the world but reassured us that we should "be of good cheer" because He has "overcome the world."[8] When we show good cheer even amid the storms of the world around us, we build our children's confidence and faith.

I remember hearing President Hinckley say on occasion, "Things will work out. They always do." As a mother, I find myself frequently repeating similar phrases: "It will be fine." "Don't worry; it will work out." "You're fine. Everything will be okay." This same kind of comfort must continue even as the waves of the storm grow louder and stronger. Our babies and toddlers become youth and then young adults, and they will still need our reassurance. President Gordon B. Hinckley pleaded with parents: "My heart reaches out to our youth, who in many cases must walk a very lonely road. They find themselves in the midst of these evils. I hope they can share their burden with you, their fathers and mothers. I hope that you will listen, that you will be patient and understanding, that you will draw them to you and comfort and sustain them in their loneliness. Pray for direction. Pray for patience. Pray for the strength to love even though the offense may have been serious. Pray for understanding and kindness and, above all, for wisdom and inspiration."[9]

As their needs move beyond our ability to heal, we must turn to the Savior for His healing power. Just like John the Baptist did for his followers, we must point them toward Jesus Christ for all of the comfort and healing they need. Our Heavenly Father, who is a perfect parent, will help us parent His children if we seek His help. The Savior's example and our own answered prayers will give us the words to say and the healing hands our children need. Elder Holland emphasized the importance of being a refuge for our children: "I can tell you this as a parent: as concerned as I would be if somewhere in their lives one of my children were seriously troubled or unhappy or disobedient, nevertheless I would be infinitely more devastated if I felt that at such a time that child could not trust me to help or thought his or her interest was unimportant to me or unsafe in my care."[10]

When we reach out to our children in the spirit of comforting and healing—in the spirit of *succoring*—we help them trust us and gain a deeper understanding of the Savior's ability to "make it better." There is something so sacred about a mother's healing role. Her gentleness reflects Jesus Christ's love and watchcare over His children.

Even as a grown woman, I know I can call my mother and receive the comfort and encouragement I seek, even on the worst of days. I have watched dear friends who are wading through deep and painful trials post a few simple words on Facebook declaring to the universe that things are going to be fine: "My mom is here." A mother can be a messenger of the peace and comfort that comes through Jesus Christ. "Peace I leave with you, my peace I give unto you: not as the world giveth, give I unto you. Let not your heart be troubled, neither let it be afraid" (John 14:27).

CHAPTER 4

# Jesus Christ Provides

IT WOULD BE NEARLY IMPOSSIBLE to count all of the things a mother does for her children on any given day, but many of those services fall into the category of providing. We feed them. We clothe them. We buy school supplies. We make treats for the class Valentine party. We keep Band-aids and Tylenol on hand. Regardless of who earns the money in the family, mothers are often the ground-level providers for children's needs. In "The Family: A Proclamation to the World," our obligation is made clear: "Parents have a sacred duty . . . to provide for their [children's] physical and spiritual needs."[1]

Jesus Christ is the perfect provider. He gives just what is needed to bless His children and help them achieve their potential. During His earthly ministry, even when resources were limited, He always managed to provide enough. Jesus' first recorded miracle was a miracle of providing. He attended a wedding where the hosts ran out of wine for their guests. At the bidding of His mother, Jesus instructed the servants to fill their vessels with water, and when they served the water to the guests, it became wine, a wine so fine, in fact, that the guests complimented the hosts on saving the best for last.[2]

Jesus called His disciples at the beginning of His ministry and did so after showing them that He could provide for their needs. He called out to Simon Peter on his fishing boat to let down his nets. Peter replied, "Master, we have toiled all the night, and have taken nothing: nevertheless at thy word I will let down the net." When they followed Jesus' suggestion, "they inclosed a great multitude of fishes: and their net brake."[3] Then they were called to leave their nets and become fishers of men.

Peter was once approached to pay money for a tribute tax. When he asked Jesus what to do, Jesus replied, "Go thou to the sea, and cast an hook, and take up the fish that first cometh up; and when thou hast opened his mouth, thou shalt find a piece of money: that take, and give unto them for me and thee."[4] And so it was. Jesus Christ continued a pattern of providing.

On another occasion, Jesus was teaching a crowd of followers, and as the day waned, they became hungry. The disciples wanted to send them away, but Jesus answered, "Give ye them to eat. And they say unto him, Shall we go and buy two hundred pennyworth of bread, and give them to eat? He saith unto them, How many loaves have ye? go and see. And when they knew, they say, Five, and two fishes." So Jesus blessed the food and commanded it to be distributed among the crowd. "And they did all eat, and were filled. . . . And they that did eat of the loaves were about five thousand men."[5] Now, I have never fed five thousand people at my table, but I've certainly faced a throng of ravenously hungry people and not known what I would provide them. Any mother who has somehow created a meal out of two or three random ingredients from her scant pantry has, on some level, participated in the miracle of the loaves and fishes.

Jesus instructed on many occasions, "Feed my sheep," or "Feed my lambs." While we often focus on missionary work or spiritual nourishment, we mothers should not overlook the straightforward opportunity we are given to feed His lambs. The miracle of the loaves and fishes was not just spiritual; it was also about a physical hunger being filled. The disciples complained to Jesus at that moment, saying, "Send them away, that they may go into the country round about, and into the villages, and buy themselves bread: for they have nothing to eat." Perhaps they saw their role as simply teachers and didn't want to bother with their audience's other needs, but Jesus understood that true ministry is providing for both spiritual *and* temporal needs. "He answered and said unto them, Give ye them to eat."[6]

President Dieter F. Uchtdorf explained the following principle:

> The two great commandments—to love God and our neighbor—are a joining of the temporal and the spiritual. It is important to note that these two commandments are called "great" because every other commandment hangs upon them. In other words, our personal, family, and Church priorities must begin here. . . . Unfortunately, there are those who overlook the temporal because they consider it less important. They treasure the spiritual while minimizing the temporal. While it is important to have our thoughts inclined

toward heaven, we miss the essence of our religion if our hands are not also inclined toward our fellowman.[7]

President J. Reuben Clark Jr. taught that Jesus Christ modeled this selfless focus: "When the Savior came upon the earth he had two great missions; one was to work out the Messiahship, the Atonement for the fall, and the fulfilment of the law; the other was the work which he did among his brethren and sisters in the flesh by way of relieving their sufferings."[8]

Mothers play a key role in this kind of ministry. Not only do we teach and "train up a child in the way he should go,"[9] but we also provide for his or her physical needs. By doing so, we create an environment where our children can learn the gospel. A quick study of the history behind the Church's welfare system indicates that the temporal needs must be met before true conversion can take place. President David O. McKay shared this experience from his own mission:

> In 1897 when I was on my first mission, I found myself, one morning, distributing tracts in a little undesirable district in Stirling, Scotland. I approached one door and in answer to the knock a haggard woman stood before me, poorly dressed, with sunken cheeks and unkempt hair. As she received the tract I offered, she said, in a rather harsh voice, "Will this buy me any bread?" . . . From that moment I had a deeper realization that the Church of Christ should be and is interested in the temporal salvation of man. I walked away from the door feeling that [she and her husband], with the bitterness in their hearts toward man and God, were in no position to receive the message of the gospel. They were in need of temporal help, and there was no organization, so far as I could learn, in Stirling that could give it to them.[10]

This experience sparked a new perspective for President McKay, and several decades later, during the Great Depression, the Church established the welfare program while he was serving as a counselor to President Heber J. Grant. Both the Church and the organization of the priesthood set forth patterns we can follow at home. In that context, then, mothers, along with their husbands, become the administrators and distributors of welfare principles within the walls of their own homes. We assess and meet the needs of our children. We feed them. We clothe them. We provide for their health and well-being. We emulate the Savior's way of feeding His sheep.

Feeding our own little lambs is no easy endeavor. I learned early on that we have a "witching hour" in my house. It's the late afternoon shift before Dad comes home when the children (and their mother) seem to be at their very worst. We're all a little tired and grumpy, but despite being tired, the children are full of energy and noise. Ironically, this is the same time of day when I usually have to make dinner. It can often feel like a chore, or at least a monumental inconvenience, to put together a meal for a small, hyper crowd; however, it can be an opportunity to show love for the Savior.

After Jesus Christ was resurrected, He appeared on the shore of a lake and called out to His apostles to "come and dine" with Him. They did not recognize Him at first, but when He advised them to cast their nets to one side of the boat, they did so, and the nets were filled to the point of breaking. They then recognized the Savior, and Peter dove into the water and swam to Him. Christ waited for the disciples with "a fire of coals there, and fish laid thereon, and bread."[11] Consider the conversation that then took place between Jesus Christ and Simon Peter:

> So when they had dined, Jesus saith to Simon Peter, Simon, son of Jonas, lovest thou me more than these? He saith unto him, Yea, Lord; thou knowest that I love thee. He saith unto him, Feed my lambs.
>
> He saith to him again the second time, Simon, son of Jonas, lovest thou me? He saith unto him, Yea, Lord; thou knowest that I love thee. He saith unto him, Feed my sheep.
>
> He saith unto him the third time, Simon, son of Jonas, lovest thou me? Peter was grieved because he said unto him the third time, Lovest thou me? And he said unto him, Lord, thou knowest all things; thou knowest that I love thee. Jesus saith unto him, Feed my sheep.[12]

There is obviously a spiritual metaphor in the Savior's plea, but the context of their fireside meal shows that He fed both body and soul. Perhaps we can remember this conversation the next time we prepare a meal, even if we are weary and surrounded by chaos. "Lovest thou me? . . . Feed my sheep."

Jesus Christ's example teaches that there is spiritual meaning tied to temporal providing. I was able to recognize a number of those patterns as I went back through my journals and read about some of the more exhausting days of my motherhood experience so far. Just to make a point, I'm including bits and pieces of actual entries to recreate a detailed, hypothetical day in the life of a young mother. Though it is a sample journal entry, I suspect it will sound painfully familiar to any mother:

*I woke up this morning to the sound of the children playing and arguing in the family room. I got up and sent them off to their respective morning chores: get dressed, brush teeth, etc. I changed a diaper and then bathed and dressed Natalie. I heated up some instant oatmeal and helped the boys get started on breakfast. While they talked and laughed (and made a mess of their breakfast), I packed their lunches for school. Once coats, gloves, shoes, and homework were finally found, I herded everyone into the car and drove the boys to school.*

*When I got back home, I wiped up the remains of oatmeal and gathered up the laundry. I sorted it and got one load started. Natalie needed attention, so I read some stories and helped her get some paper and crayons for coloring. She lost her temper about something (crayon broke or wrong color) and ended up screaming and crying. When she wouldn't be comforted, she lashed out at me and landed herself in time-out. After a few minutes, I went and talked to her and hugged her, and she was free from time-out, and resumed making messes wherever she went.*

*I switched over another load of laundry. I left the clean clothes in a pile on the couch in hopes of getting to them later. It was time for lunch. Hot dogs. There were no clean forks in the drawer, so I got some from the dishwasher and made a mental note to unload it soon. We ate, and Natalie went down for a nap. I added one more clean load to the couch pile and moved another load from the washer to the dryer.*

*I thought about lying down while the baby was sleeping, but when I walked past the bathroom, I saw the toilet full to overflowing with almost an entire roll of toilet paper. After staring at it in disbelief for a while, I came back with tongs and a plastic grocery bag and did my best with the damage. Then I restocked the bathrooms with toilet paper, carried the garbage out to the curb, and called Matt at work to tell him about the toilet adventure. He mentioned he had a homeowners' association meeting that night. He forgot he was supposed to take some refreshments, and could I make something?*

*I looked around on the food-storage shelves and gathered a few ingredients to make cookies. Just as I was getting ready to put them in the oven, I heard crying upstairs. I went up to check on Natalie, and she was flushed and sweaty. I felt her forehead, and it seemed warm, so I took her temperature. Great, 99.9, I thought. Looks like we're headed for sickness. Again.*

*I gave her some fever-reducer and held her on my hip while I finished the cookies. Once the timer beeped, I pulled them out of the oven and ran off to pick up the boys from school. We came back home, and I started homework supervision. Natalie was fussy and kept wanting milk in her sippy cup, so I kept refilling between times tables and tracing letters and thinking about what in the world I was going to make for dinner. Homework finally done, I scooted over the laundry piles so the boys could watch a show. They argued about what to watch, so I just picked something myself.*

*Natalie's fever kept rising, and knowing her chronic health history, I called the doctor to see if I could get her in for a urinalysis. They had an opening, but it was at the same time as Grant's flag football game. I called Matt to see if he could meet me at the game and stay there with the boys so that I could run Natalie to the doctor. He agreed, and I had everyone get ready so we could head out the door in a few minutes.*

*Grant reminded me that we were in charge of snacks for his game, so I hurried them even faster so we could stop at the store on the way. No stop at the grocery store is ever quick when you have three children in tow, but we picked up our juice boxes and crackers and loaded and buckled ourselves back into the car as quickly as we could. Husband met and the boys dropped off, I made my way to the doctor's office. The urine tested positive for bacteria, so we were given a prescription, and we headed to the pharmacy. I still didn't know what was for dinner, and that load of laundry was still in the washer. We managed to get home before the boys, and I threw some pasta on the stove and heated up some vegetables. Matt and the boys got home, and we all ate.*

*I helped all of the children get ready for bed. The boys took baths, and we read scriptures. I gave Natalie her medicine and put on her pajamas. We read stories, and I tucked them all in and turned off the lights. I went downstairs and found that Matt had cleared the dishes before he left for his meeting, so I put away the leftover food and cleaned the table and counters. I thought about folding laundry, but I got on the computer and worked on my sharing time lesson for Sunday for a little while. I checked e-mail and Facebook, and finding myself tired, got up to go to bed.*

Now, let's imagine that after a day like this, a day that surely rings familiar to many mothers, I went to bed, settled down into my pillow, and remembered I still needed to read scriptures. I opened to Matthew 25:34–40, where Jesus Christ is speaking to His disciples:

> Then shall the King say unto them on his right hand, Come, ye blessed of my Father, inherit the kingdom prepared for you from the foundation of the world:

For I was an hungred, and ye gave me meat: I was thirsty, and ye gave me drink: I was a stranger, and ye took me in:

Naked, and ye clothed me: I was sick, and ye visited me: I was in prison, and ye came unto me.

Then shall the righteous answer him, saying, Lord, when saw we thee an hungred, and fed thee? or thirsty, and gave thee drink?

When saw we thee a stranger, and took thee in? or naked, and clothed thee?

Or when saw we thee sick, or in prison, and came unto thee?

And the King shall answer and say unto them, *Verily I say unto you, Inasmuch as ye have done it unto one of the least of these my brethren, ye have done it unto me.* (Emphasis added)

These verses are a testimony to me that all of the details of a mother's day—no matter how mundane and unimportant they seem—are expressions of love to our Savior. We are doing His work. Sister Silvia H. Allred testified: "The pure love of Christ is expressed as we give selfless service. Helping one another is a sanctifying experience which exalts the receiver and humbles the giver. It helps us become true disciples of Christ. The welfare plan has always been the application of eternal principles of the gospel. It truly is providing in the Lord's way."[13]

On the rare occasions when I feel on top of my game and properly balanced—like the landmark achievement of three solid meals, clean clothes, completed homework, and wholesome family activities all in the same day—I fantasize about my children sitting around in the future reminiscing about the joy and comfort of their perfect childhood. All joking about elusive perfection aside, one of the greatest things we provide for our children is a legacy. We can give them memories and traditions and testimony that they will pass on from one generation to the next.

One mother wrote her own conclusions about the right kind of legacy:

Because we live in a time when social forces have attempted to devalue women's work in the home, a widespread misperception is that the only valuable contributions to be made to society have a paycheck attached to them. . . .

We must never lose sight of the fact that our efforts and time spent in rearing our families in the safe refuge of gospel-centered homes are our most lasting legacy of all. . . .

Latter-day Saint women have a unique perspective on building homes: we build them for eternity, understanding that the efforts we make today can reap rewards forever.[14]

Jesus Christ provides, and so do mothers. We keep our covenants with Him by consecrating our time and energy to building up His kingdom, starting first with our homes. That covenant relationship blesses us and our families, and we come closer to Him by emulating His work.

## Chapter 5
## Jesus Christ Cleanses

CLEANING IS PERHAPS THE MOST repeated and most wearisome task among all of a mother's efforts—the dishes, the laundry, the bathing and wiping, and the constant picking up and tidying the house. I myself have often used the phrase "shoveling snow in a blizzard" to try to communicate the futility of it all to my husband. Almost immediately upon cleaning, we witness entropy as the messes return. Even more common among those of us with crawlers and toddlers and hyperactive young children, we diligently clean one area to our satisfaction only to walk out and find that the rest of the house has been destroyed in the meantime. It can feel incredibly frustrating, and we often want to throw our hands in the air and surrender.

I can only speak from my own experience, of course, but on one such occasion, I began to gain insight that has helped me see things differently. As I have already mentioned, there were four years where my husband worked full time during the day and then attended law school at night. My oldest child was three when this phase in our lives began, and my second son was close behind at two years old. During my husband's first-semester finals, our daughter was born, bringing the total to three children ages three and under. Though much of the next four years was a blur, I'm proud to say that we all survived. There were moments when I wondered if we would.

I was so tired, and every time I turned around, there was something or someone that needed to be cleaned. I remember an inner dialogue that would often surface: *Seriously? I am a bright and intelligent woman. I have a master's degree, for heaven's sake. I am blowing noses and vacuuming Cheerios and scraping spit-up off of car-seat buckles. Is this seriously how I'm supposed to spend my life?* Maybe I am exceptionally shallow or slow . . . or normal. I'm not sure, but while I know there are some mothers out there who find joy all along the journey of motherhood, I struggled to find meaning in what I was doing day in and day out. I admire those other mothers; I really do.

I found joy in *being* a mother because I loved my children. I knew being a mother was important and right and part of God's plan for me. That much I knew, and I didn't doubt my choice, but I could not wrap my head around all of the mind-numbing details of my motherhood reality. Was there really meaning in all of that? What was I missing? These feelings ignited a desire in me to understand motherhood more, to recognize the value in what I was doing more than just in a long-term sense. I began to study and pray about it and think about it. Think about it *a lot*.

I learned that Heavenly Father cared a great deal about how I felt about motherhood. He wanted me to see it how He sees it, so He started to show me. One afternoon, I was sitting on the floor in my daughter's room, changing her soiled diaper. I removed it, cleaned her, and fastened on a fresh diaper. The following scripture came into my mind: "Though your sins be as scarlet, they shall be as white as snow" (Isaiah 1:18). It dawned on me that Jesus Christ was in the cleaning business. A crucial part of His mission was taking things or people that were soiled and making them clean. In that moment, I felt a flow of love and revelation—clusters of thoughts and ideas that started to fit together like a puzzle. My job was a reflection of His. It could teach me about Him and make me more like Him. This was life-changing information.

Jesus Christ is a cleanser, both temporally and spiritually. He was once invited to dine in the home of a Pharisee. While there, He was visited by a "woman in the city" who brought a beautiful alabaster box full of ointment, threw herself at His feet, "and began to wash his feet with tears, and did wipe them with the hairs of her head, and kissed his feet, and anointed them with the ointment."[1] When the Pharisee objected, knowing what a sinner the woman was, Jesus taught an important lesson:

> And he turned to the woman, and said unto Simon, Seest thou this woman? I entered into thine house, thou gavest me no water for my feet: but she hath washed my feet with tears, and wiped them with the hairs of her head.
>
> Thou gavest me no kiss: but this woman since the time I came in hath not ceased to kiss my feet.
>
> My head with oil thou didst not anoint: but this woman hath anointed my feet with ointment.

> Wherefore I say unto thee, Her sins, which are many, are forgiven; for she loved much: but to whom little is forgiven, the same loveth little.
>
> And he said unto her, Thy sins are forgiven.[2]

Not only did He acknowledge and appreciate her gift of washing, but He washed her clean in return by forgiving her sins. The New Testament is full of examples where the Savior healed and blessed and made people whole by saying, "Be thou clean." The physical healing was a symbol for the spiritual healing that came by way of being washed clean through His Atonement. He cast out unclean spirits, forgave the sinners, and cleansed the lepers.

When a crowd of neighbors came across a man who was obviously cured of his blindness, they were amazed and asked about the source of his healing. He answered and said, "A man that is called Jesus made clay, and anointed mine eyes, and said unto me, Go to the pool of Siloam, and wash: and I went and washed, and I received sight."[3] Jesus Christ used washing as a powerful tool to change people for the better and to help them understand His mission.

Anyone who has ever been unclean—whether by accident or as the natural result of contact with dirty elements—knows the great relief that comes after a warm bath or cleansing shower. Dirty is uncomfortable; clean is refreshing. It's no wonder then that the act of helping another to be clean is an act of service. Carefully consider this account of what Jesus Christ Himself did for His disciples just hours before Gethsemane, perhaps as a foreshadowing of the greater cleansing service to come:

> He riseth from supper, and laid aside his garments; and took a towel, and girded himself.
>
> After that he poureth water into a bason, and began to wash the disciples' feet, and to wipe them with the towel wherewith he was girded.
>
> Then cometh he to Simon Peter: and Peter saith unto him, Lord, dost thou wash my feet?
>
> Jesus answered and said unto him, What I do thou knowest not now; but thou shalt know hereafter.
>
> Peter saith unto him, Thou shalt never wash my feet. Jesus answered him, If I wash thee not, thou hast no part with me.
>
> Simon Peter saith unto him, Lord, not my feet only, but also my hands and my head.

Jesus saith to him, He that is washed needeth not save to wash his feet, but is clean every whit: and ye are clean, but not all.

For he knew who should betray him; therefore said he, Ye are not all clean.

So after he had washed their feet, and had taken his garments, and was set down again, he said unto them, Know ye what I have done to you?

Ye call me Master and Lord: and ye say well; for so I am.

If I then, your Lord and Master, have washed your feet; ye also ought to wash one another's feet.

For I have given you an example, that ye should do as I have done to you.

Verily, verily, I say unto you, The servant is not greater than his lord; neither he that is sent greater than he that sent him.

If ye know these things, happy are ye if ye do them."[4]

When my son Clark was six years old, he taught our family home evening lesson about service. He bore his testimony at the end of his lesson: "So if you know you should do service but you really don't want to because you just don't feel like doing service, even if someone tells you to, you still have to do it. Because service equals love." At the time, when I had been feeling weary about some of my mothering duties, the Holy Ghost reminded me of the lesson I had learned earlier that year: When I struggle, I need to pray to love what the Lord loves. When I see the love, I see the joy.

We discussed the service we do for each other in our family, and Clark said, "If Mom was gone from our family, that would be horrible. I would starve to death." He told us all to draw a picture of service, and then we showed them to each other. When my husband held up his picture, he said (pointing to the right side), "This is mommy putting socks in the washing machine," and (then pointing to the left), "This is Jesus washing the feet of His disciples." The kids all giggled at his artwork, but I understood what he meant, and I loved him for it. After all, Jesus taught, "Follow me, and do the things which ye have seen me do."[5] Cleaning equals service, and service equals love.

On that diaper-changing afternoon where I started to learn about the meaning of my service, my mind was filled with ideas about covenants and how those covenants are fulfilled and reflected in small ways in our lives. When we make a covenant with our Heavenly Father, we make a promise and become eligible for greater blessings. Often, those covenants are associated with ordinances, and often, those ordinances are associated with signs and tokens that stand as symbols and reminders of the covenant we have made. As evidence of this principle, after Noah and his family survived the flood, God placed a rainbow in the sky and explained: "This is the token of the covenant which I make between me and you and every living creature that is with you, for perpetual generations: I do set my bow in the cloud, and it shall be for a token of a covenant between me and the earth. And it shall come to pass, when I bring a cloud over the earth, that the bow shall be seen in the cloud: And I will remember my covenant."[6]

It is a fascinating study to look up the words *sign* and *token* in the topical guide, read the indicated scriptures, and realize how often our Heavenly Father provides us with symbols that remind us of Him and His promises. When we take the sacrament each week, the bread and water are tokens of our Savior's body and blood. When we see them, touch them, and partake of them, we are reminded of Jesus Christ and the fulfillment of His covenant with us to take away our sins.

As we remember His promises, we have the opportunity to draw closer to the Savior and renew *our* promises with Him. Ordinances in the holy temple are also laden with symbolism that represents sacred vows. The temple garment, for example, is a token of temple covenants. As such, the garment functions as a daily sign of the Lord's promised protection and the covering power of His Atonement. Just like the sacrament reminds us of our baptismal covenants, the garment reminds us of our commitment to keep specific temple covenants and demonstrates our respect for the laws of God. When we wear it regularly as commanded, it draws our attention to Him and to the temple, and we have a recurring opportunity to remember and renew our promises.

Elder Russell M. Nelson taught, "Children of the covenant have the right to receive His doctrine and to know the plan of salvation. They *claim* it by making covenants of sacred significance."[7] Such covenants, like the ordinances of sacrament and temple worship, are rituals we participate in repeatedly. What I began to understand is that some of the other simple things we do every day can likewise teach us about the doctrines of Jesus Christ. The fact that they are repeated often, even daily or hourly, helps them function as tokens in our lives.

Each time I change a diaper or wash dishes or wipe a face or give a bath or make dirty laundry clean, I can be reminded of my covenant relationship with Jesus Christ. He promised me that "though [my] sins be as scarlet, they shall be as white as snow,"[8] and I know He "loved [me], and washed [me] from [my] sins in his own blood."[9] Elder D. Todd Christofferson said, "It becomes clear that spiritual rebirth originates with faith in Jesus Christ, by whose grace we are changed. More specifically, it is faith in Christ as the Atoning One, the Redeemer, who can cleanse from sin and make holy."[10]

Elder Clate W. Mask Jr. gave a talk in general conference called "Standing Spotless before the Lord," where he related an account about a group of missionaries who had to push a bus through the mud in order to arrive at zone conference on time. Using this as an example of how we all sometimes encounter the mud of sin in our life's journey, he testified, "Because of the Atonement of Jesus Christ, we can all stand spotless, pure, and white before the Lord. . . . May we thank our Father daily for sending us His Son, Jesus Christ, to forgive us our mud spots so that we may stand spotless before Him."[11]

My simple service of cleaning in my own home and with my own family mirrors His greater mission. It makes me love Him more, know Him more, serve Him more, understand Him more, and even become more like He is. And when I think of all the times I sin and repeat the sin or fall into new ones, I realize that I am not much different from my children and their messes; nevertheless, Jesus Christ cleanses me over and over and over again because He loves me. Cleaning equals service, and service equals love.

Having said all of the above about the powerful symbolism behind cleaning and serving, I need to make a sincere disclaimer: I don't think we're supposed to have a perfectly clean house. Sometimes covenant women hear talks and counsel about how our homes should be like the temple. We somehow imagine that our living room is supposed to look like the celestial room. This is a ridiculous standard to hold ourselves to; after all, children are not allowed in the temple, and no mortal being lives there.

Our home is a temple, not because it looks like one but because of the eternally important work that happens there. We teach and learn the gospel there. Our home is a temple because it is a refuge from the world and because we can feel love there. Mothers are the temple matrons of their homes, but they cannot possibly maintain a celestial room atmosphere at all times. I think we're supposed to *want* a clean house and work toward it as a worthy goal, but we should be more gentle with ourselves and our children when we can't maintain perfect order.

In general conference, I heard the following statement about Mary and Martha's house: "It was a welcome place for the Master, where He could rest and enjoy the surroundings of a righteous home."[12] I believe the Savior would rather visit a home where people are working together harmoniously (even in a very unfinished project) than a home where a mother on the verge of a nervous breakdown is screaming at her children to get their dishes off the table, and they better not have left the hand towel on the floor after they used the bathroom.

In fact, if He showed up at my house, I'd bet He would sit on the floor next to me and help me fold laundry while we talked about important things. But I'd miss out on that if I ran around anxiously trying to clear the counters and make the beds before I paid Him any attention. I think I'd even miss out on that if I sat down with Him with my mind constantly focused on everything that was undone. Sister Cheiko N. Okazaki expressed a similar sentiment:

> Suppose the Savior were to come visit you. You've rushed around and vacuumed the guest room, put the best sheets on the bed, even placed some tulips in a vase on the dresser. Jesus looks around the room and says, "Oh, thank you for inviting me into your home. Please tell me about your life." You say, "I will in just a minute, but something's boiling over on the stove, and I also need to let the cat outside."
>
> Jesus says, "I know a lot about cats and stoves. I'll come with you."
>
> "Oh, no," you say. "I couldn't let you do that." And you rush out, carefully closing the door behind you.
>
> While you're turning down the stove, the phone rings, and then Jason comes in with a scrape on his elbow, and the visiting teacher supervisor calls for your report, and then it's suppertime, and you couldn't possibly have Jesus see that you don't even have placemats on the table, and someone forgot to turn on the dishwasher so you're eating off paper plates, and then you have to drive Lynne to her basketball game. By the time you get back to the room where Jesus is waiting patiently, you're so tired that you can barely keep your eyes open, let alone sit worshipfully at his feet waiting for words of profound wisdom and spiritual power to wash over you, to make you different, to make everything else different, and you fall asleep whispering, "I'm sorry. I'll try to do better. I'm so sorry."[13]

Perhaps we need to invite Him to trudge along through our day. What He won't do *for* us by way of chores, He will certainly supplement with His encouragement and companionship if we let Him. Please don't misunderstand. I still believe "cleanliness is next to godliness," and all of that "house of order" stuff, but I believe what matters most is that we are consistently striving to make our home a place where the Spirit of God is welcome. And if that's our goal, be it in the early stages of chaos or the last load of laundry, for all intents and purposes, I think the Savior knows He's invited. And that's all that matters.

Motherhood is certainly busy. Amid all of the teaching and loving and healing, we somehow have to find the time to do all of the cleaning and providing. But it all testifies of Jesus Christ. It all makes us better. Elder Dallin H. Oaks said of Christ:

> What do members of The Church of Jesus Christ of Latter-day Saints think of Christ?
>
> Jesus Christ is the Only Begotten Son of God the Eternal Father. He is our Creator. He is our Teacher. He is our Savior. His Atonement paid for the sin of Adam and won victory over death, assuring resurrection and immortality for all men.
>
> He is all of these, but he is more. Jesus Christ is the Savior, whose atoning sacrifice opens the door for us to be *cleansed* of our personal sins so that we can be readmitted to the presence of God. He is our Redeemer.[14] (Emphasis added)

I'm so thankful for Jesus Christ, and even though the cleaning and serving can sometimes feel wearisome, I know it is His work on a smaller scale. If cleaning is meant to be a symbol of His Atonement, how could it possibly be *easy* to do? It may never be my favorite activity, but that's okay. It is a token of His love for me; it is an honor to have the opportunity to be reminded of Him every day.

## Chapter 6
# Jesus Christ Defends and Protects

MOTHERS HAVE A NATURAL INSTINCT to protect their young. I remember one time when my son Clark was just learning to read. We were standing in line at the grocery store, and there he was, eye level to all of the trashy magazines, with their pornographic photos and headlines. I asked the check-out lady to call the manager for me, and she did. I made him walk with me to the aisle and showed him where my son's line of vision was. I said, "I don't know if you have children of your own or not, but I think you can agree that this is not appropriate reading material for a child." I asked him to either move the magazines out of sight, like they do with cigarettes, or cover them up. I told him that I'm probably not the only mom who would appreciate a safe shopping environment for my children.

He replied by saying that the magazine distributor was actually there in the store restocking the shelves, and he went to talk to her. He asked her to put shields over the front of the inappropriate magazines, and she agreed. I continued my grocery purchase and the cashier said, "I'm a sixty-nine-year-old woman, and even *I* find some of that stuff offensive." I walked out of there feeling like a superhero, and that feeling returned every time I shopped there and saw those magazines covered up.

Even though there's always a small part of me that wants to save the world, the real motivation is born from the fact that I have children I want to protect. The outcome isn't always that glorious. I've spoken to managers at different stores for similar reasons and been treated with contempt and total dismissal. But my career—my motherhood—demands that I protect the children I've been given, and I will.

The perfect example in all things, Jesus Christ, was a consummate defender. He repeated on several occasions, "How oft would I have gathered you as a hen gathereth her chickens under her wings."[1] He protects His own and fights bravely against the enemy. I love the story of Jesus cleansing the temple of the moneychangers. Think of the temple as a symbol for sacred space, like our home, our family, or our stewardship, and then consider this account from the New Testament: "And they come to Jerusalem: and Jesus went into the temple, and began to cast out them that sold and bought in the temple, and overthrew the tables of the moneychangers, and the seats of them that sold doves; And would not suffer that any man should carry any vessel through the temple. And he taught, saying unto them, Is it not written, My house shall be called of all nations the house of prayer? but ye have made it a den of thieves."[2]

When it came to protecting that sacred space Jesus called "my house," He didn't hold back. As a mother who struggles a little bit with anger, I've always appreciated this passage because it gives me a context for when anger or passion are appropriate. Oftentimes, anger is used in destructive ways to a spouse or children, but here, Jesus shows our obligation to *defend* our homes and families. In fact, He gave a stern warning about the importance of keeping children safe: "But whoso shall offend one of these little ones which believe in me, it were better for him that a millstone were hanged about his neck, and that he were drowned in the depth of the sea."[3]

One thing I love about Jesus Christ is how He stands up for people. When His disciples came across a blind man on their path, they wondered out loud whether he was a sinner or whether his father and mother were sinners. Jesus explained to them, "Neither hath this man sinned, nor his parents: but that the works of God should be made manifest in him,"[4] and then He healed him.

When the woman caught in adultery was brought before Christ and the captors wanted to stone her to death, Christ never joined in their accusations but treated her with dignity and respect. He said, "He that is without sin among you, let him first cast a stone at her," and when the accusers' pricked consciences caused them to drop their stones and walk away, He gently encouraged, "Neither do I condemn thee: go, and sin no more."[5] He saved lives, but He also kindly watched over people. I try to teach my own children about our family obligation to protect one another. After a related family home evening lesson, I put up a large version of the following saying on our family room wall, where it still remains:

*This is a safe home.*
*People are safe.*
*Feelings are safe.*
*The Holy Ghost is safe.*

What do we protect and defend? Safety, the Spirit, and feelings. As mothers, we are the front line in defending our families from the influences of the world. In her talk called "Protecting and Nourishing the Family," Sister Julie B. Beck pointed out that our families face a *spiritual* threat due to current trends in society: "Let's review briefly some of the things that are threatening the family. In Ephesians chapter 6, it says, 'We wrestle not against flesh and blood, but against principalities, against powers, against the rulers of the darkness of this world, against spiritual wickedness in high places' (verse 12). That is what we are fighting against. . . . We are in those times when we are the ones who must preserve our families amid the gathering evil around us."6

Jesus Christ also declared that our greatest concern should be for spiritual and eternal welfare: "And fear not them which kill the body, but are not able to kill the soul: but rather fear him which is able to destroy both soul and body in hell."7 This is not an easy time to be a parent because it is not an easy time to be a child. Elder Jeffrey R. Holland called it a time when "it seems that a sea of temptation and transgression inundates [our children], simply washes over them before they can successfully withstand it, before they should have to face it. And often at least some of the forces at work seem beyond our personal control."8

Because this is such a wicked world, I am so grateful for living prophets and apostles who help us navigate our way safely through the traps and snares that Satan has set for us and for our families. I feel a personal responsibility to help my children gain a testimony of these men and their messages, so we try to make general conference a big deal at our house. I know these men we sustain as prophets, seers, and revelators are truly watchmen on the tower, and their counsel will keep our families safe against the evils of the day.

Even I was surprised when my five-year-old, Natalie, recently asked me to guess what her favorite holiday was. I guessed Christmas.

"Nope," she said. "Christmas is number two. What's number one?"

I didn't know.

She smiled and said, "General conference."

"Really?" I asked.

"Yep."

Then she listed some of her favorite general conference traditions, like treats while listening for key words, our fun conference notebooks, identifying each speaker on a picture chart, and enjoying special meals together. That was a payback moment for me as a mother. President Henry B. Eyring testified that heeding the words of the prophets protects us: "There seems to be no end to the Savior's desire to lead us to safety. And there is constancy in the way He shows us the path. He calls by more than one means so that it will reach those willing to accept it. And those means always include sending the message by the mouths of His prophets whenever people have qualified to have the prophets of God among them. Those authorized servants are always charged with warning the people, telling them the way to safety."[9]

These prophets, apostles, general authorities, and auxiliary leaders have repeatedly warned about the attacks we are facing and the urgent need to protect our families. Any efforts we make, any defenses we put in place, any battle where we stand our ground—all are a fulfillment of this charge and a reflection of our covenant relationship with our Heavenly Father. Sister Sheri L. Dew shared an experience that helped her better understand a mother's protective role:

> Four teenage nieces and I shared a tense Sunday evening when we set out walking from a downtown hotel in a city we were visiting to a nearby chapel where I was to speak. I had made that walk many times, but that evening we suddenly found ourselves engulfed by an enormous mob of drunken parade-goers. It was no place for four teenage girls, or their aunt, I might add. But with the streets closed to traffic, we had no choice but to keep walking. Over the din, I shouted to the girls, "Stay right with me." As we maneuvered through the crush of humanity, the only thing on my mind was my nieces' safety.
>
> Thankfully, we finally made it to the chapel. But for one unnerving hour, I better understood how mothers who forgo their own safety to protect a child must feel. My siblings had entrusted me with their daughters, whom I love, and I would have done anything to lead them to safety. Likewise, our Father has entrusted us as women with His children, and He has asked us to love them and help lead them safely past the dangers of mortality back home.[10]

When we parent for protection, we emulate the mission and ministry of Jesus Christ; His covenants often echo the promise that He will protect His covenant people. Modern-day prophets and apostles have exhorted us to protect and defend our families—the people with whom *we* have covenant relationships. And it is not surprising that they teach us to start in the home. A home is often compared to a temple, but it is also a bunker, a place of refuge from the battle that surrounds us and our children. President Spencer W. Kimball said:

> To be a righteous woman is a glorious thing in any age. To be a righteous woman during the winding up scenes on this earth, before the second coming of our Savior, is an especially noble calling. The righteous woman's strength and influence today can be tenfold what it might be in more tranquil times. She has been placed here to help enrich, protect, and guard the home—which is society's basic and most noble institution. Other institutions in society may falter and even fail, but the righteous woman can help to save the home, which may be the last and only sanctuary some mortals know in the midst of storm and strife.[11]

When the stripling warriors went out to battle, it was not military training that made them successful; the truths they had been taught *in their homes, by their mothers*, gave them the strength and protection they needed. While our children's enemies today do not usually present a physical threat with swords and bows and arrows, there are some necessary ingredients to prepare for the kind of defense our children *do* need, as outlined by President Boyd K. Packer:

> We can also protect our children from moral and spiritual diseases. . . .
>
> The Book of Mormon gives us the key:
>
> ". . . Feast upon the words of Christ; for behold, the words of Christ will tell you [and your children as well] all things what ye should do" (2 Ne. 32:3).
>
> If you will accept it in your mind and cradle it in your feelings, a knowledge of the restored gospel and a testimony of Jesus Christ can spiritually immunize your children.
>
> One thing is very clear: the safest place and the best protection against the moral and spiritual diseases is a stable home and family. This has always been true; it will be true forever. We must keep that foremost in our minds. . . .
>
> This shield of faith is best fabricated in a cottage industry. While the shield can be polished in classes in the Church and in activities, it is meant to be handcrafted in the home and fitted to each individual.[12]

When my son Grant was in the second grade, he had his first incident with a bully. I could tell something was wrong, but I had to ask a few questions before the whole truth came out. Even then, it took a couple of days before he was ready to tell the story. I learned that when the "lioness at the gate"[13] finds out one of her cubs is getting knocked around, she doesn't feel very docile at all. But since a lioness wandering the halls of elementary schools swiping at naughty children with her claws and growling at unobservant teachers is kind of frowned upon, I had to take a more civil approach. All of this stemmed from Grant's having been verbally insulted at school. He didn't really understand if the word being used to describe him was a true label or not.

Talking about it openly and honestly helped him gain a much clearer picture of himself and his own feelings. I was shocked that some of these issues came up at such a young age, but they did. Thank heaven for the gospel of Jesus Christ. When I can draw upon the scriptures and the family proclamation and the teachings of living prophets to help my children navigate this crazy world they live in, I feel adequately armed. I am sometimes scared, but I'm so glad I know I can call on divine help.

I can give my children a proper context and framework for all they see, hear, and feel. I can share my testimony and express confidence in them. I can say, "You can come talk to your dad and me about anything, and we will listen. We (you and us together with God's help) will find the answers." I can plead with Heavenly Father to help me understand their little hearts and help me say the right things. And He hears me and helps me. The First Presidency declared that by teaching and rearing children in gospel principles, parents can protect their families from corrosive elements.[14] Oh, how we need that protection!

We can do this. We are covenant mothers in Zion. Sister Virginia U. Jensen, who served as a counselor in the general Relief Society presidency, expressed her confidence in us: "Sisters, I do not believe that you and I are here at this unique time by accident. I believe that, like Esther of old, we are 'come to the kingdom for such a time as this' (Esth. 4:14), when our influence, our example, our strength, and our faith may stand as a bulwark against the rising tide of evil that threatens to engulf our homes, our families, and our loved ones."[15]

The greatest comfort to me is knowing that my children are not mine alone. They are His, and the scriptures testify over and over again that He protects His children. Even in a wicked world where the forces seem beyond our control, the Lord will help us lead our children to safety. Elder David A. Bednar taught about preventative measures parents can use to access both protection and direction in our own lives and in the lives of our children. He recommended reading and talking about the Book of Mormon, bearing testimony to our children spontaneously, and inviting them to act upon the principles they learn. By doing so, we invite the following promised result: "The spiritual discernment and inspiration you will receive from the combination of these three holy habits will enable you to stand as watchmen on the tower for your families—'watching . . . with all perseverance' (Ephesians 6:18)—to the blessing of your immediate family and your future posterity."[16]

When as parents we fret about our children's safety and pray fervently to know how to protect their bodies, their tender feelings, and their spirits, we can remember that this effort is an opportunity to be and to act more like our Savior. Like He did, we can turn to our Father in faith and offer up our own best efforts. We can provide a defense for them with the teachings of truth and the refuge of our homes. By drawing our children to the Savior, we introduce them to the best protector of all.

## Chapter 7
# Jesus Christ Loves and Sacrifices

LOVE AND SACRIFICE HAVE A reciprocal relationship. When we truly love someone, we are willing to sacrifice for them. We sacrifice our selfishness, our will, our time, sometimes even our desires and preferences. On the flip side, sacrifices that we make for others deepen the bond we feel with them. I have been surprised by the fortitude of a mother's love. There are days when I almost feel like I'm battling my children—their arguing, disobedience, disregard, and disdain are relentless. I become exasperated and discouraged, but then the day ends. I tuck them into their beds, the night falls, and peace reigns. Sometimes I go back into their rooms and look at their gentle faces and watch the rise and fall of their rhythmic breathing. Even after a day that would leave any other occupation in serious jeopardy, my mother heart swells. And I love them. It's an irrational love because it almost doesn't make sense in the context of the day's events. But I just *love* them.

It seems that mothers love their children with a special kind of love, and I think mother love is one of the most profound ways we emulate Jesus Christ. Our children disobey, and we love them anyway. They oppose us, and we love them anyway. They wear us out and sometimes dreadfully disappoint us, and we love them anyway. Mothers make mistakes, of course; we do and say things we regret, but in the end, the love remains—a residual reflection of what our Savior feels for us. It is unconditional love.

Our children, without even trying, teach us how to love like our Father loves us. When Jesus offered the great intercessory prayer, He pleaded to His Father on behalf of all of His disciples, "That they all may be one; as thou, Father, art in me, and I in thee, that they also may be one in us: that the world may believe that thou hast sent me. And the glory which thou gavest me I have given them; that they may be one, even as we are one: I in them, and thou in me, that they may be made perfect in one; and that the world may know that thou hast sent me, and hast loved them, as thou hast loved me."[1] Perhaps we are blessed with families in order to learn and to cultivate this same kind of unity and love—to experience devoted relationships in such a way that our eternal happiness is intrinsically connected to theirs and we are, therefore, willing to make sacrifices in exchange for the well-being of those we care for.

It might be wise to mention that our children need *not* be asleep to cause feelings of love to stir within us. Days and weeks are often full of ordinary events, but there are magical moments when we feel overcome with love. These moments are not necessarily extraordinary, but sometimes our feelings are. Elder M. Russell Ballard described the phenomenon like this: "Recognize that the joy of motherhood comes in moments. There will be hard times and frustrating times. But amid the challenges, there are shining moments of joy and satisfaction."[2]

Several years ago, my boys were sitting on the couch and Grant was helping Clark read the words to a library book he had just recently learned to read himself. He was being patient and encouraging and kind. Clark was happy. Natalie toddled over and climbed up on the couch to join them, plopping herself into a sunbeam on the cushions. She hugged her sippy cup and was happy to be near them. Clark finished the book triumphantly, jumped up, and hugged his brother. "Thank you, Grant!" They smiled. It was a capsule of happiness in the middle of a regular day, and we all felt it. That was a happiness I could not feel with anything else, and I felt grateful for them and grateful for my chance to be a witness to all of the future ups and downs of their human development.

Another day, two days before Grant's first day of kindergarten, I overheard this conversation between my boys while they were coloring pictures at the kitchen table:

Grant: "I can't wait to wake up tomorrow because I'm going to be even *more* excited!"

Clark: "Grant, are you so excited to go on the bus?"

Grant: "Yep. See you soon, Clark."

Clark: "I'll miss you every day when you're at kindergarten."

Grant: "I'll miss you too, Clark. But don't worry. I'll be fine at school."

Clark: "I can't believe in a week, I go to *my* school with Mrs. Sue." [Referring to preschool]

Grant: "Mrs. Sue is nice, Clark. She has curly hair, and sometimes she has a purple shirt."

Their sweet dialogue reminded me of the Savior's words: "A new commandment I give unto you, that ye love one another; as I have loved you."[3] Children teach us a lot about how to love people and comfort one another. I wonder why we adults are sometimes slower to express our affection for each other and quicker to diminish other people's fears and worries. It's no wonder that when Isaiah prophesied about the coming days of peace, he said, "And a little child shall lead them."[4]

We read in the Book of Mormon that when the resurrected Jesus Christ appeared to the Nephites, the whole congregation experienced an indescribable outpouring of the Spirit as He interacted with the children. He wept as He looked upon them. Jesus prayed words so powerful that it was impossible for them to be recorded. He blessed the children one by one, and then He turned to their parents and said, "Behold your little ones."[5] Angels came down from heaven and surrounded the children as by fire, and the multitude was overcome. I sometimes wonder, *What did the Savior see in those children that I often fail to see in my own?* He must know so much more about them than what we see. Elder Ballard explained: "Notice that He didn't say 'glance at them' or 'casually observe them' or 'occasionally take a look in their general direction.' He said to *behold* them. To me that means that we should embrace them with our eyes and with our hearts; we should see and appreciate them for who they really are: spirit children of our Heavenly Father, with divine attributes. When we truly behold our little ones, we behold the glory, wonder, and majesty of God, our Eternal Father."[6]

We know that charity is "the pure love of Christ."[7] I have often thought that in order to have charity, we must learn to see people as the Lord sees them and then love them as He loves them. Moroni taught that charity is a gift we should pray to obtain. Therefore, in our prayers to love what the Lord loves, we should remember to ask for His help to love *whom* the Lord loves and to love *how* He loves. Brigham Young taught, "We should commence our labors of love and kindness with the family to which we belong; and then extend them to others."[8] In this way, motherhood helps us emulate the Savior's love in our own homes and become—little by little—as charitable as He is to all mankind.

"The Family: A Proclamation to the World" gives mothers a charge to be nurturers. As the world becomes more and more hardened, we must make our homes places where children can see love and hear love and feel love. God *is* love,[9] and our children will not know Him if they cannot feel His Spirit. President Spencer W. Kimball taught, "There is a constant need to develop and to maintain tenderness. . . . The tenderness of our women is directly linked to the tenderness of our children."[10] Referring to nurturing, Sister Julie B. Beck taught that "mothers who know create a climate for spiritual and temporal growth in their homes."[11] This is one more important way our homes can be like a temple: at home, we feel God's love.

Jesus Christ's ministry teems with examples of love. It appears that He shared His love most often through service, kindness, compassion, attention, and succoring. In fact, all of the different roles of His ministry are manifestations and expressions of His love.

As we fulfill our roles as mothers and emulate these different aspects of the Savior's ministry, we both give and receive His love. When we and Jesus create, we show love. When we teach, we do so out of love. We protect and succor and heal because of love. When we provide and when we clean, we give evidence of our love.

Service stretches and deepens our love. Neither the Savior's love nor our own can be whole without sacrifice. From the earliest moments of motherhood, we begin to give of ourselves in the love and care of another soul. Consider the following evidences of sacrifice, even from the very beginning: as an embryo grows and develops, a mother gives away some of her own nutrition, energy, comfort, and, in some cases, general health in the process of nurturing. During the travail of childbirth, a mother literally enters into "the valley of the shadow of death,"[12] and for the sake of a child, she is "wounded" and "bruised."[13] Through "the Spirit, and the water, and the blood,"[14] she gives life. It is no mistake that these things represent Jesus Christ; as a woman turns mother she becomes a symbol of the Savior.

The symbolism of sacrifice continues once a baby enters a mother's life. Whether by birth or by adoption, that baby changes her world. Life as she has known it is completely redefined by the ever-growing and ever-changing needs of her child. Some things that were once essential in her life now fall completely off the radar. Things she never before considered important suddenly score high on her list of priorities. A child is born, and the woman is reborn. I love what President Spencer W. Kimball said about the sacrifices a mother makes and how those sacrifices make us who we should become: "One of the important messages that emerges from the history of great women in all ages is that they cared more for the future of their families than for their own comfort. . . . Selflessness is a key to happiness and effectiveness; it is precious and must be preserved as a virtue which guarantees so many other virtues. . . . It was never easy to bear and rear children, but easy things do not make for growth and development."[15]

The world today celebrates the concept of love when it meets individual needs but discounts the personal growth that comes through sacrifice. The battle cry of individualism is "Find yourself," rather than the Savior's call to lose ourselves in the service of others and, surprisingly, thus fulfill our emotional and spiritual needs. There is a growing opinion that the price of motherhood is far too inconvenient to pay. The sad result of this sentiment is a society that increasingly fails to invite God's children into the world and then forgets to honor the mothers who make that brave choice. I feel inspired by the idea that the difficult choice to bear and raise children actually facilitates our becoming the person our Heavenly Father designed us to be.

This balance between sacrifice and the ability to give and receive love played an important role in my own journey into motherhood, and I believe that many women navigate the same dilemma. Motherhood was not an easy choice for me; it required what felt like significant surrender. Growing up, I never had one of those spiral notebooks where you glue in pictures of wedding dresses and swatches of fabric for your future bridesmaids' colors. I don't think I was a particularly morose or lonely child; I just didn't fantasize about marriage, and certainly not about motherhood. I had a hard time picturing myself married, and my limited experience with babysitting hadn't unlocked some latent desire to birth and diaper babies. I couldn't picture myself cleaning a house and whistling songs. I couldn't picture myself loving somebody enough to want to be with them more than I wanted to do anything else or be anything else.

I used to think that mothers should be patient and kind all of the time. I also thought people chose to be moms because they *loved* all of that kid-related stuff, like playdates at the park and making your own baby food and baking cookies for the PTA. Now that I'm all grown up, I realize that probably only about 1.7 percent of the population is well equipped to automatically be a great mother. The rest of us just kind of muddle through it somehow, regardless of the obvious deficiencies in our résumés or character.

My life *has* turned out differently than I'd imagined. Despite the fact that my dating years were mostly frustration dabbled with moments of humiliation, unrequited admiration, and my own episodes of Mormon-girl soap opera, I eventually found love. One of the most remarkable things about falling in love was the discovery of a completely different kind of future than I'd pictured for myself. The right person can make a woman see herself doing things she never dreamed possible. Sometimes, like in the case of having children, I never dreamed it would be desirable, but Cupid worked his magic, and just like Dr. Seuss's Grinch, my heart grew two sizes. Love slowly began to breed sacrifice.

Making the decision to start a family is no small matter. It's possible to know that something is the right thing to do and still be scared out of your mind. I never had cold feet about marrying my husband, but I fearfully tiptoed on the threshold of motherhood for years. I had faith in God, and I knew He loved and honored children and families, but I didn't have faith in myself. I still stupidly thought I had to be "qualified" to be a mother. One day, I realized what was probably already obvious to all of the people who knew me or who had taken the leap themselves: *You'll never be ready.* I stopped fighting it, and we moved forward.

Now I have three children who complete me. If my teenaged self had had any idea how much I would love these loud, dirty, and hyperactive little monsters, she would have started that spiral notebook and let herself dream. I wish I could have helped her understand that what felt like sacrifice was really the most direct pathway to giving and receiving love. These children have torn me down with sleepless nights and singing in annoying voices in the car and spilled canisters of brown sugar and the artful placement of unknown substances in my carpets and on my walls. The miracle though, is that by tearing me down, they've somehow managed to rebuild me into something I never knew I could be.

I am a mother.

I try to be patient and kind, and I have *maybe* about a 50 percent success rate. I'm not fond of playdates, because I'm still not very good with other people's children. I never once made my own baby food, unless you count smashing up whatever was on my plate at the Cheesecake Factory. I don't think I've ever made anything for a bake sale, but I was the secretary on the PTA board for one year. I've somehow managed to shatter most of the stereotypes I believed about motherhood. I do it my own way, and it only works for one simple reason: God helps me.

Elder Jeffrey R. Holland spoke about the challenges of the young mother and then testified: "Do the best you can through these years, but whatever else you do, cherish the role that is so uniquely yours and for which heaven itself sends angels to watch over you and your little ones. . . . Mothers, we acknowledge and esteem your faith in every footstep. Please know it is worth it then, now, and forever."[16]

My Heavenly Father lets me try again and again to get it right when I get it wrong. And I do get it wrong, and I do try again. When I have a day full of frustration and, yes, sometimes despair, He blesses me with a moment of joy or a glimpse of clarity, and I know I am doing what He made me for. Even when I lose my temper because I find all the clean clothes I just folded "put away" in the dirty laundry hamper or when I get food off the pantry shelf to make dinner and find the hidden wrappers of forbidden treats or when I spend forty-five minutes trying to convince my daughter that "my shoes feel funny" is not a sufficient reason to stay home from preschool, there is still a reassurance that it all counts. It counts for their good. It counts for my character. It matters to God.

He uses all of those opportunities to teach me the value of sacrifice—of selflessness—in learning to love deeply. My whole life has become a collection of simple moments, the kind of moments that my young self could never appreciate. In fact, a lot of people who consider themselves educated and capable adults don't appreciate it either. But like many truths, the truth about the divine role of women is often buried in the details of daily living and goes mostly unnoticed by the world at large.

I used to dream really big. My notebooks were more about traveling the globe and getting degrees and teaching and making a difference. I'm happy to report that over time the Lord has blessed me with chances to do many of those things, but not one of them matters to me as much as the people He gave me. God and my little family have turned me into a better me than the me I had imagined. And when all is said and done, if I were to find out that I wasn't allowed to keep most of the things that are important to me, my husband and children are the things I would hold on to the tightest. The things I never knew I wanted are my greatest treasure.

This union of sacrifice and blessings bears a strong witness to me of Jesus Christ's words: "He that findeth his life shall lose it: and he that loseth his life for my sake shall find it."[17] After all, the Son of God understood better than any of us the important relationship between love and sacrifice: "Greater love hath no man than this, that a man lay down his life for his friends."[18] It's no wonder that the patterns of motherhood can so powerfully draw us toward Jesus Christ. As we see our children as He sees them, love them as He loves, and sacrifice for them as He did for all of us, we share in His work and prepare ourselves to be even as He is.[19]

## CHAPTER 8
# Jesus Christ Forgives and Shares Burdens

JESUS CHRIST'S ENDLESS MERCY IS perhaps the most difficult of His attributes to emulate; however, the relationship mothers have with their children gives us insight into the connection between love and mercy. When we love a child deeply, we are quicker to offer second chances. Our love increases our willingness to endure with them in times of struggle. Our mother hearts measure children by their potential rather than by their mistakes and trials, and we rejoice with them when they overcome weaknesses. It stands to reason that Christ's infinite mercy springs from His infinite love.

During the course of children's development, they make the same mistakes over and over and over again. A loving parent does not condemn the child for the mistakes, lose hope, or give up on the child. On the contrary, we try to correct errors, reteach principles, and give the child opportunities to be successful. In this way, we model our Savior's plan of mercy and help our children come to know and understand His love and forgiveness because they have experienced ours.

Not only does Jesus Christ offer to exonerate us from our mistakes, He also offers His help as we navigate the pain and sorrow those mistakes bring. He is ready and willing to bear any burden we experience as part of our mortal experience, whether it comes through sin or simply the human condition. In fact, He took upon Himself all of our sins, as well as our "pains and afflictions and temptations of every kind"[1] when He suffered the Atonement in the Garden of Gethsemane and upon the cross. Emulating the Savior Himself, mothers' hearts are tied to their children's hearts; mothers share in their children's suffering, and they share in their joy. Most importantly, they share in Jesus Christ's ministry and purpose.

My son Clark is a parable for all human beings. He wants to be good, but he makes a lot of mistakes. He is impulsive, adventurous, and often acts without thinking. He has completely mastered the art of whining. He makes a monumental mess out of most things he tries to do, and he beams with pride when he gets things right. His most repeated phrases are, "Sorry, Mommy," and "Oops, I forgot."

One afternoon during his preschool years, he declared at lunch, "I'm going to try really, really hard to never, ever be naughty again," and I couldn't help but smile. I love the kid to death, but it didn't take a rocket scientist to figure out he'd be in time-out again by midafternoon. But you know what? I loved that he wanted to be good. I loved that he knew what that meant and that in his heart, he wanted to do it. And as I thought about his declaration, a flash of inspiration entered my mind, and I made a big connection.

Heavenly Father is a loving, believing parent too. He honors our *desire* to do what's right. He knows we'll mess up (we always do), but He completely loves us anyway and keeps teaching us the same lessons over and over again. He has faith that we'll figure it out and get our act together. He believes in us so much that He even sacrificed His beloved Son to make it possible for us to change everything for the better. And when we say, "Oops, sorry," He sincerely accepts the apology and moves on. I am confident that Clark will turn out just fine, and I'm encouraged to think that God just might feel the same way about *me*.

Jesus Christ offers us the pattern of how this forgiveness and mercy should be extended. Almost every healing and miracle He performed was accompanied by a declaration of forgiveness. The lepers, the blind, the lame, and the halt were cleansed and renewed in both body and spirit. The adulterous woman, though caught "in the act," was not condemned by the Savior but was sent away with the charge to "go, and sin no more."[2] When the young man, sick of the palsy, was lowered down through the roof of a building so Jesus could heal him, not only was he told to "arise, and take up thy bed, and walk," but, to the shock of the observing scribes, he was told, "Son, thy sins be forgiven thee."[3] And the woman who interrupted Christ's feast to bathe His feet in oils and tears was also told that her sins were forgiven. Some were outraged at the immediate acquittal of someone so unclean, causing Jesus to tell the dinner guests the parable of the debtor, wherein He declared, "To whom little is forgiven, the same loveth little."[4]

Jesus also clearly taught the principle of forgiveness in His sermons and conversations. On one occasion, "came Peter to him, and said, Lord, how oft shall my brother sin against me, and I forgive him? till seven times?"

The Messiah's answer came as a surprise after centuries of the Mosaic law, wherein each infraction required quick and equal justice: "I say not unto thee, Until seven times: but, Until seventy times seven."[5] He reinforced these same principles during the Sermon on the Mount, teaching His disciples to love their enemies, speak not in anger, pray for those that take advantage of them, and turn the other cheek.[6]

Metaphors like the mote in the neighbor's eye versus the beam in our own eye further emphasize the importance of focusing on our own sins and not withholding forgiveness from others.[7] Finally, in the Doctrine and Covenants, the Savior pointedly lays out our responsibility regarding mercy: "I, the Lord, will forgive whom I will forgive, but of you it is required to forgive all men." He even adds this stern warning: "He that forgiveth not his brother his trespasses standeth condemned before the Lord; for there remaineth in him the greater sin."[8]

Jesus Christ taught us to forgive, so each time we extend mercy, we are following His example and becoming more like He is. I have already mentioned that I believe there are lessons to be learned in the banal duties of motherhood. Those signs and tokens point us to Christ and His purpose. For example, the laundry cycle is actually what mortality is all about. Clean clothes come out of the dryer and then they get dirty again. I clean them, and they get dirty again. I gather them up, clean them, and they get dirty again. You get the point.

We are all like laundry. We try so hard to be good, but we make mistakes and start over again and again, maybe even seventy times seven. God forgives us, and we are clean, but it doesn't take long before we need Him to help us clean up our act again. We have to repent often, and like that time when I got mad at my cousin Darren and pinched him just a few minutes after I was baptized, I rarely manage to maintain the purity of His cleansing forgiveness. This reinforces for me a few important things about Jesus Christ:

> 1. He is far more patient with me than I am with myself, or with my dirty laundry for that matter.
> 2. I need Him. A lot. And often. Thank goodness for the sacrament and its continuous access to the cleansing Atonement.
> 3. I will never finish my laundry, but He will finish me. I can eventually become perfected in Him; that's His promise. It gives me a whole new perspective on the scripture that calls Him "the author and *finisher* of our faith."[9]

A few years ago, I listened carefully to all of the messages at the general Relief Society broadcast and loved President Dieter F. Uchtdorf's talk. He told us to focus more on what we do right and less on what we do wrong. He said we are too hard on ourselves and should celebrate what we accomplish even if it's not perfect.[10] It was a great reminder.

One morning shortly thereafter, Clark was working on writing his lowercase letters at the table. I went into the bathroom to brush my teeth, and I could hear his frustration mounting. "Mommmmyyyyy . . . I'm not doing it right. It's *not* working!" I spit out my toothpaste and called out, "It's okay to make mistakes when we're learning, Clark," and I was struck by the profundity of my own statement. In light of President Uchtdorf's message, it clicked for me. *Hello? I'm just learning how to be a mother.* Granted, I was already five years into it and probably should have figured out a little bit more by then, but I am literally a perpetual student of motherhood.

I will make mistakes. Those mistakes are okay if I really am learning. Do I have a desire to do it right, and am I practicing? Clark made lowercase *R*s that looked like *N*s many more times until he figured it out, but no big deal. He learned it. He *got* it. And so will I. Isn't that exciting? We really should give ourselves more credit. We can have confidence that the same mercy and patience we extend to our children will also be extended to us.

Interestingly, our children are often the most Christlike example of forgiveness. Mine are frequently the victims of the mistakes I make as a mother, and there have been many times when I have had to ask their forgiveness. Even as I wrote this book, I had a humbling experience that required me to repent and refocus. I had been working hard on editing and research and then left my office to talk on the phone with a friend who needed advice. The conversation drew long, and I returned to my desk to find something that took my breath away. Natalie had drawn her five-year-old version of a computer on a piece of red cardstock, complete with a keyboard and mouse. There was a big, wobbly circle around it with a diagonal line, the universal symbol for "Don't," and in her little writing at the top of the page were the words, "No Mom!" It was taped to my keyboard. I felt a snap in my heart. I had failed my daughter, and she wanted me back.

I tearfully found her, and we talked about her note. I told her I was so sorry and reassured her that she meant more to me than my work on the computer. We agreed to a system that would allow me some writing time while she did her chores and guaranteed playtime for her when she was done. It was a heartbreaking moment for me. I felt the keen irony of ignoring my child while I wrote a book about motherhood, but she extended all the love and mercy and patience I did not deserve. A quick hug, a game of princess Chutes and Ladders, and all was forgotten. Her mercy helped me become a better mother, and so does our Redeemer's.

Mercy can facilitate healing. Like Jesus Christ does for us, we offer forgiveness and mercy to our children, and sometimes that mercy extends to the realm of sharing their burdens. All loving mothers feel pain when their children suffer. Sister Sheri Dew said, "The subject of motherhood is a very tender one, for it evokes some of our greatest joys and heartaches. This has been so from the beginning. Eve was 'glad' after the Fall, realizing she otherwise 'never should have had seed'[Moses 5:11]. And yet, imagine her anguish over Cain and Abel. Some mothers experience pain because of the children they have borne; others feel pain because they do not bear children here."[11]

President Gordon B. Hinckley also acknowledged how closely a mother's feelings are tied to her children. Speaking to mothers, he said, "They are His children and they are your children, flesh of your flesh, for whom He will hold you responsible. You have rejoiced over them, and in many cases you have sorrowed. They have brought you happiness as no one else could. They have brought you pain as none other could."[12]

The first time I remember feeling anguish over a child was when my son Grant was two years old and had a series of several unexplained seizures over the short course of a day. He was rushed to the hospital, where doctors performed several tests. Both the tests and the doctors' questions made us realize there were some seriously frightening possibilities. As I watched Grant suffer more seizures with the confused doctors looking on and then later when I held him in my arms while he came out of heavy narcotics, I felt like my heart would break. It was almost more than I could bear. There was an ache and a fear I had never before experienced. Grant was suffering, and so was I.

Then, several years later, I found myself in the waiting room at an urgent care facility with Natalie in my arms. Just minutes before, I had stepped out into the hall at church and the bishop had told me Matt was looking for me because Natalie was not well.

When we found each other, Matt said, "Natalie has a fever, and she needs to go home."

She didn't look good, and she had tremors.

"Something's not right," I said.

I took her, started asking for directions to the nearest urgent care, and headed out immediately. She was hot and listless, and I felt scared. I know most people don't react to fever like I do, but after spending three days in pediatric intensive care with a son whose violent seizures were concluded to be somehow related to a low fever, I respond a little differently.

So with my eyes frequently darting to the rearview mirror, I drove quickly and offered many prayers in my mind. I took Natalie out of the car, and she was still very feverish. I checked her in, and the nurses asked all of their regular questions. I knew I didn't land on their "must be seen quickly" list by their reaction to my description, so I added, "I just know something is not right." We waited for about fifteen minutes before Natalie started crying out again. She threw up all over her lap and mine. I sat stunned, not knowing where to move or what to do next. A nice man brought me a garbage can, and I threw her tights away after I used the dry half of them to wipe us off a little. After that, she fell asleep with her steamy little head on my chest. When she stirred after awhile, I was able to get a small hospital gown and change her out of her soiled dress.

I sat holding her for a long time after they checked her vitals. The rise and fall of her hot little body against mine made me feel a tight bond to her; her health was just as much a part of me as my own. My mother mind went through all of the worst-case scenarios, and I mourned each one and ached for her. I sometimes have days where I fantasize about spending some nice quiet time away from my children for a while, but in that moment, I had a strong impression that gave me a new awareness. I realized I would rather be there in that urgent care room, covered in vomit, *with her*, than be anywhere else in the world, including a beautiful white and sunny beachfront *without her*. I would not have traded the love I felt for her for any of the "freedom" my life might have had without her. God gently reminded me how much I need my children.

It took several days and several other visits to the doctor's office, but my persistence paid off, and they found she had a urinary tract infection that could have threatened her kidneys. This has been a chronic condition for her, and she still struggles with it years later, despite surgery and several other medical endeavors. Regardless of the familiarity with her condition, each time she gets sick, I hurt for her and with her, and I wish I could take her pain away.

Sometimes the burdens mothers bear with their children are longer lasting and deeper reaching. Even though we want to fix everything or make the struggles go away, we frequently cannot, and we must follow the example of Jesus Christ, who shares burdens by strengthening us and by walking with us and lightening our load. He invites, "Take my yoke upon you, and learn of me; for I am meek and lowly in heart: and ye shall find rest unto your souls."[13] This is a part of His mission that mothers emulate often—sharing our children's stress and sorrow. When our children experience painful or difficult circumstances, we participate in this yoke metaphor as we walk the hard road with them and help relieve their suffering.

A mother's love and support emulate the charitable burden-sharing Christ offers all of Heavenly Father's children. Our baptismal covenants require us to "bear one another's burdens that they may be light; Yea, and [be] willing to mourn with those that mourn; yea, and comfort those that stand in need of comfort."[14] Motherhood certainly gives us plenty of opportunities to do just that. Only the Savior Himself can truly heal our children, take their sins, and be their ultimate source of strength, but we mothers can model His love and compassion and mercy. A mother's willingness to help her child bear a burden can help that child trust the Savior's love.

Sometimes burden-sharing manifests itself in simple ways. For example, any mother knows that when a child has schoolwork, Mom's workload increases too—not because we do the work but because we have to remind and encourage and organize and supply and somehow maintain the sanity of all involved parties. Recently, Grant began to struggle in school, and I became frustrated. He forgot about assignments, failed to turn in work that he had done, and didn't bring home everything he needed to complete his homework. The more I tried to push and correct him, the less he responded to my help. It became a battle, and things seemed to get worse rather than improve. I didn't want to take over his responsibilities, nor did I want to leave him to his own resources because he was floundering, so we had to figure out a way to work together and share the load—to be yoked in the process. I asked him what I could do to help him. He came up with some ideas of things *he* could do better. We met with his teacher and enlisted her help as well. The teamwork lessened the pressure he felt. We are doing better now, but I still need to patiently walk with him while he gains the strength and skills to do more on his own.

In today's age of entitlement and helicopter parenting, it's important to remember that sharing burdens does not necessarily mean removing them. I taught high school for a time, and that gave me a front-row seat to both extremes on the spectrum of parental involvement. The patterns I saw have spiritual implications as well. Sometimes there is a tendency to step in, fix any problem, and save the child from any failure. In the context of the yoke metaphor, the parent either marches forward and drags the effortless child or doesn't even give the kid the dignity of strapping on the yoke at all. That lopsided parent-child relationship does not build the strength the child will eventually need as the loads and burdens of life increase.

Other times, parents are detached from their children's lives, challenges, and endeavors. There is danger in relying too heavily on our children's agency and not offering the guidance and support they desperately need. In these cases, the child heaves the yoke unaided and may fall short of his potential. A child carrying a yoke alone has a hard time walking straight. Remember that the Savior said, "Come unto me, all ye that labour and are heavy laden, and I will give you rest."[15] What Jesus Christ does for us is so beautiful and simple. He expects us to work and to try, and He encourages and helps us along the way. We still face difficult challenges. We suffer, but He promises that He will never leave us in times of trouble. "For the mountains shall depart and the hills be removed, but my kindness shall not depart from thee."[16]

Helping Grant navigate his school responsibilities is a simple thing, but it teaches him that I will support him, and it teaches me what the Savior will do for me. My children are still young, and there are undoubtedly more painful experiences ahead. I am thankful for the example of friends who have shown me that even when the challenges are daunting, mothers can share their children's burdens and follow the example of Jesus Christ. These friends keep the covenants they have made with Him as they mourn with and comfort their children. When we have talked on the phone or sat across from each other over lunch or spilled the contents of our hearts in the gym parking lot, I have been so impressed with the lessons that have come through their merciful mothering. They would not call it that because, to them, it is simply being a mom and doing what is required, but I see reflections of the Savior in their stories. Different mothers face different challenges, and no one story can be universal, but their experiences show a pattern of dependence upon the Lord and loving service toward children that can apply to a variety of circumstances.

My friend Amy has a daughter who was born almost fifteen years ago with a chromosomal defect that has left her both physically and mentally delayed. Megan has all the sweetness and innocence of a toddler wrapped up in the body of a Mia Maid, and while she is full of love and spirit, her care has not always been easy. Amy explained that her first instinct and one that comes often is to just wish it away, to make everything "normal," mostly for Megan's sake. Amy mourned the handicaps because she knew Megan would have to struggle, face rejection, and probably miss out on the blessings of marriage and motherhood.

The lesson Amy has learned repeatedly is that, despite her longing to remove the obstacle, it has been placed there for those who come in contact with Megan. Amy, her husband, and their four other children have all learned more about Jesus Christ because of their association with Megan. Amy compares her journey with Paul's sermon about the "thorn in the flesh."[17] Like Paul, when Amy wishes that Megan could be free of her struggle, she recognizes God's hand in it. Paul doesn't want it taken away anymore, and he glories in the suffering because of what it helps him learn.

Amy has relied heavily on the doctrine of grace and has told me that, for her, "grace is the power to do something you feel like you can't." Whenever she feels like she can't do her mothering for even another minute, she draws on that grace and relies upon it to carry her through the minute she can't do on her own. Referring to the analogy of the Savior sharing His yoke, she explained that He doesn't take the burden away, but He carries it *with* her. This is exactly what she does for Megan. Her mother heart basically says, "Let's figure this out and do the best we can together."

She knows that with each child, her job is to assist them in reaching *their* potential. Amy reads Megan books and sings her songs because Megan loves those things but doesn't have the skills for them. She gives grace the same way she receives it, doing for Megan what Megan can't do for herself. One of the lessons she's learned in the giving of grace is that sometimes Heavenly Father lets us struggle a little so we learn what we *can* do, but the help always comes when we need it. In this and in so many other ways, Amy is a Christ-symbol in Megan's life and in mine.

In small and simple ways, in the ins and outs of our daily mothering, we create a loving and merciful bond with our children, and we share in their suffering because of that love. That same love allows us to share in their joy, and that helps us—and them—better understand our Savior's love for us.

Jesus Christ testified that He will forgive us as often as we will repent. He has covenanted to receive us by extending His mercy. He helps us bear our burdens so we do not carry them alone. Our role as mothers is a reflection of our covenant relationship with Jesus Christ, and as we too extend mercy and offer a yoke of support, we help our children come unto Him.

## Chapter 9
## Jesus Christ Saves

THE MOST SIGNIFICANT TASK OF the Savior's mission is a role that He, and He alone, could fulfill. As the foreordained Messiah and the Only Begotten Son of the Father, He performed the Atonement for all mankind, and "there is none other way nor name given under heaven whereby man can be saved in the kingdom of God."[1] Only Jesus Christ can cleanse us from sin and conquer death. In all of the many roles of His ministry and mission, we have been able to draw parallels with our role as mothers, and the business of saving souls is no exception. A child who suffers, for whatever reason, triggers a parent's suffering, and the act of bearing a struggling child's burden often requires parents to practice ransom and deliverance. While it clearly is *not* within our power to forgive sin or take away the effects of the Fall, mothers and fathers *do* work together to bring souls back to their Father in Heaven, and many times those efforts include rescuing.

Countless righteous parents throughout history, beginning as far back as the preexistence, have seen their children wander from the path of truth. God Himself watched a portion of His spirit children walk away from His plan when it was presented to them. He continues to witness sorrow and suffering among His earthly children whose choices are contrary to His guidance. Our very first mortal parents, Adam and Eve, faced the willful disobedience of a child, and every generation since has had its share of wayward children. Even the most dedicated and attentive parents have experienced the mourning and longing that accompanies the spiritual loss of a child. But parents can follow the example of Jesus Christ and become "saviors on Mount Zion"[2] for their own posterity.

The scriptures provide anecdotal evidence that good parents are not immune to struggling children. Lehi and Sariah, Alma, Noah, Isaac and

Rebekah, Jacob and Rachel, Helaman, and King Mosiah are just a few examples that come to mind. Jesus Christ testified that His whole mission was about rescuing those who are lost: "And this is the Father's will which hath sent me, that of all which he hath given me I should lose nothing, but should raise it up again at the last day,"[3] and "For the Son of man is come to seek and to save that which was lost."[4]

In Luke chapter 15, Jesus Christ taught about the importance of seeking out what has been lost. He gave the parables of the lost sheep, the piece of silver, and the prodigal son. In the first parable, we read the story of a shepherd who leaves the ninety and nine sheep in an effort to find the one missing sheep. Upon finding it, he carries it back on his shoulders and rejoices with his friends. In the second parable, a woman loses a piece of silver and searches for it into the night, even lighting a candle and sweeping the whole house. She too calls her friends and neighbors to celebrate when she finds it.

After both of these parables, Jesus testified that the angels in heaven rejoice each time a sinner is found and a soul is rescued. Finally, the parable of the prodigal son tells the beautiful story of a father who joyously welcomes home his son after a long period of riotous living and wasted inheritance. He runs to embrace his son and throws a feast to honor his return to the family. "For this my son was dead, and is alive again; he was lost, and is found. And they began to be merry."[5]

Parents are often called upon to follow these parable patterns of seeking and saving the lost. My friend Sheri experienced an intense lesson about the Savior and His saving power when her son Derek found himself fighting a battle with substance abuse. He had become detached and apathetic and was drastically underperforming in school. In his own words, "My loving parents watched me as I headed for an epic crash and burn, and luckily, they intervened."

Sheri and her husband, along with their extended family, united in an effort to save Derek and give him every opportunity to come to himself.[6] Once, he arrived home late after what he described as "a bad trip." He was disoriented, shaking, and afraid for his life. He went to his room and fell into his bed. Throughout the night, Sheri felt helpless, but she remained by his side, rubbing his back, trying to offer comfort. He settled into rest just before dawn.

She spent her whole night offering the only thing she had to give: her presence, her love, and her reassuring touch. She gave all this despite her own deep sorrow. Another day, when circumstances continued to crumble, Sheri collapsed against the doorframe, racked with overwhelming grief, and wept in violent sobs. She ached for all that he was suffering and all that he could eventually lose because of his choices. Sheri literally felt the pain of her son's burden.

Much like Heavenly Father, Sheri could see the long-term consequences of the chosen path and desperately wanted Derek to have all the blessings available to him. He didn't see or understand what he was losing, but she did. Her mourning went beyond what he himself could mourn because her understanding of what the future could hold was far greater. She realized her own willingness to do anything in her power to help save her son.

Everyone who loved Derek wanted to sacrifice something to help save him. They pooled their resources to invest in his healing. Sheri emphasized many times the joy she felt at being able to rescue him, gratefully acknowledging the near-miraculous circumstances that allowed them to pay for his treatment program, including mortgaging their debt-free home. She had always felt that the home had been given to them from the Lord, and to be able to use it in that way created a sense of literally *paying the price* for Derek's sins. This Atonement symbol made their investment feel sacred; it was a heavy price, made possible by the Lord's gifts, to save a soul.

Sheri recounted that as they wrote each other letters during Derek's wilderness treatment program, Derek's letters progressed from bitter to humble to grateful. She could see that he truly had come to himself. The similarities to the parable of the prodigal son did not end there. Sheri wrote the following about their experience in picking up their son:

> They told us, "Your boys are just on the other side of that hill." Gingerly, we climbed the hill and made our way down the trail. Once we rounded the bend, I caught sight of the boys, and my heart just about leaped right out of my chest. At that moment, it felt exactly like the account of the prodigal son in the book of Luke:
> 
> "But when he was yet a [little] way off, [we] saw him, and had compassion, and ran, and fell on his neck, and kissed him" (Luke 15:20).
> 
> My arms would not, could not, let go of him, and my chest would not stop heaving up and down as I sobbed my love and gratitude right onto his shoulder. We just held each other like that for what seemed like forever. . . .

He almost seemed born again—not necessarily in the Christian sense but in the sense that he had been stripped of his old life and was beginning a new one . . . one where he had discovered exactly who he is and what his purpose is—like his whole mind and body had been cleansed by the dirt and the rain and the wind and the sun and let his soul shine through like never before.

Sheri and Derek's story is rife with symbolism of our Savior, but so is every mother's. Even in small ways, we reach out to our children to try to help them find their way home. Lessons from the scriptures, the perfect example of Jesus Christ, and teachings from modern prophets and apostles have helped me recognize that there are important efforts parents can make to actively rescue their wayward children. We apply the teachings and example of Jesus Christ when we do the following for our lost children:

1. Love them
2. Pray for them
3. Cleave unto our covenants

*Love them.* When children choose a path of sin, covenant parents feel a deep sense of loss and disappointment. It is easy for the pain to translate into anger or punishment, but that energy is best invested in love and rescue efforts. Elder Robert D. Hales counseled, "We must never, out of anger, lock the door of our home or our heart to our children. Like the prodigal son, our children need to know that when they come to themselves they can turn to us for love and counsel."[7] Specifically referring to struggles with immorality, Elder John K. Carmack stated, "Parents may wonder how to be generally supportive of their young adult without condoning specific immoral behavior. Harsh and judgmental reactions, threats to disown them, or other mistreatment of such a son or daughter do not help. Parents need to continue to extend loving concern to the young man or woman while upholding God's law of chastity and morality."[8]

These same principles can be applied to any category of sin to which our children may fall prey. Our love and mercy will help them trust the love and mercy of a Heavenly Father. It is important to note that mercy does not call for a surrendered tolerance of unacceptable behavior, because "an important element of doing the best we can as parents is to provide loving but firm discipline. If we do not discipline our children, society may do it in a way that is not to our liking or our children's."[9]

Parents can express love the same way Jesus expresses love for us—through sacrifice, words, gentleness, kindness, and service. I remember hearing the story of a mother whose son was making choices that led her to despair. Their relationship was strained almost to the point of not speaking. Every night after her son was in bed, she would go into his dark room and whisper that she loved him. Only years later when he came to himself did he express to her that he had lain awake at night waiting to hear her express her love. Eventually, that love became a force for him to move toward repentance.

Love also includes hope—hope for the child and faith *in* the child. Elder Robert D. Hales shared his own beautiful testimony about the power of that rescuing hope:

> If someone in your family is wandering in strange paths, you are a rescuer, engaged in the greatest rescue effort the Church has ever known. I testify from personal experience: There is no failure except in giving up. It is never too early or too late to begin. Do not worry about what has happened in the past. Pick up the phone. Write a note. Make a visit. Extend the invitation to come home. Don't be afraid or embarrassed. Your child is Heavenly Father's child. You are about His work. He has promised to gather His children, and He is with you.[10]

*Pray for them.* Almost all of the scripture stories about parents with struggling children include some account of the parents' fervent prayers. In some cases, those prayers resulted in angels or other forms of divine intervention on behalf of the children. While our answers may not be as dramatic, the scriptures testify to the fact that a parent's prayers are heard and answered. Elder Jeffrey R. Holland asserted, "Keep praying. Those prayers will be heard and answered in the most unexpected hour. God will send aid to no one more readily than He will send it to a child—and to the parent of a child."[11]

Maybe it's because our family is extra disorganized, but we lose things around our house all the time. A few years ago, Grant was late for a baseball game, and we couldn't find his hat. After a long, frustrating search, Grant offered up a prayer. We immediately knew where to look, and we found the hat. Not too long ago, I lost my car keys. I looked everywhere I could think of without success. Finally, as a family, we said a prayer and everyone set off looking in different directions. A few minutes later, I heard Clark's voice coming from my bedroom. "I found them!" We all ran into the room and found Clark, beaming, holding my keys in his hand. He explained that after the prayer was over, he could see in his mind my gray vest, so he went to my closet, found it on a hanger, and looked in the pocket. And he found the keys.

I believe these little experiences with lost and found have served to build my testimony. I trust in Heavenly Father's willingness to answer prayers, and maybe more importantly, I know He cares about things that are lost. If my keys or Grant's hat matter to Him, then surely the much more important souls of my children are under His watchful care. Alma declared, "Yea, cry unto him for mercy; for he is mighty to save."[12]

*Cleave unto covenants.* In Doctrine and Covenants 25, the Lord gave a revelation for Emma Smith. Emma was not inexperienced in losing children.[13] Though Emma lost most of her children to death, the Lord's promises to Emma of restoration apply to all forms of rescue covered by the Atonement, especially when covenants are kept. He counseled Emma, "Wherefore, lift up thy heart and rejoice, and cleave unto the covenants which thou hast made."[14] Why are covenants so important? Not only do they allow us access to the Atonement of Jesus Christ and the resulting qualification for exaltation, but they also bind us to our ancestors and our posterity. Covenants are the glue of eternal families.

Several years ago, I sat across the table from a dear friend who was hurting. Her child had recently revealed a struggle with same-sex attraction, and she was devastated. I think her greatest fear was loss: the loss of her dreams for him, the loss of his future, maybe even the loss of his soul. She was afraid he would become lost to the family, the Church, and worst of all, to the Lord. Since the majority of my own children were still in diapers, I was in no position to give her wise counsel, but I felt the Spirit influence my conversation with her. I felt strongly that I should testify to her that the best thing she and her husband could do for their child, and for all of their children, was to keep their covenants. Those covenants are the greatest protection against losing a child.

That experience led me to study more carefully the binding power of covenants, and I am now convinced that, other than the Atonement itself, there is no more beautiful doctrine in the gospel of Jesus Christ. Orson Whitney shared a similar testimony:

> The Prophet Joseph Smith declared—and he never taught a more comforting doctrine—that the eternal sealings of faithful parents

and the divine promises made to them for valiant service in the Cause of Truth, would save not only themselves, but likewise their posterity. Though some of the sheep may wander, the eye of the Shepherd is upon them, and sooner or later they will feel the tentacles of Divine Providence reaching out after them and drawing them back to the fold. Either in this life or the life to come, they will return. They will have to pay their debt to justice; they will suffer for their sins; and may tread a thorny path; but if it leads them at last, like the penitent Prodigal, to a loving and forgiving father's heart and home, the painful experience will not have been in vain. Pray for your careless and disobedient children; hold on to them with your faith. Hope on, trust on, till you see the salvation of God.[15]

Despite whatever thorny path the child may have to tread, and the heavy weight of justice he may have to pay, the child can be brought back to us and to our Father through the power of sealing covenants.

The covenant relationship with my husband and children becomes more sacred to me when I realize that it draws upon the power of the Good Shepherd to reach out to the one and bring them back into the fold of God. My obedience to my covenants binds Heavenly Father to the promises of those covenants. My family can truly be sealed for eternity.

Referring to these covenant relationships carried out in righteousness, Brigham Young claimed, "I care not where those children go, they are bound up to their parents by an everlasting tie, and no power of earth or hell can separate them from their parents in eternity; they will return again to the fountain from whence they sprang."[16]

Parents suffer as their children wander, but this doctrine of restoration through covenants is so beautifully comforting and reassuring. Parents truly do not parent alone; the hand of God is guiding our families, and His promises will all be fulfilled. President Boyd K. Packer taught, "We cannot overemphasize the value of temple marriage, the binding ties of the sealing ordinance, and the standards of worthiness required of them. When parents keep the covenants they have made at the altar of the temple, their children will be forever bound to them."[17]

Jesus Christ atoned for me, for you, and for all of His children, including *our* children. He alone can exact within each individual a change of heart, a powerful forgiveness, and access to eternal life. However, as parents, we participate in His saving work by reaching out to our children who are lost and drawing them back into the eternal fold of Heavenly Father's family. We love them. We pray for them. We keep our covenants. We help *save* them. President Lorenzo Snow proclaimed, "Inasmuch as we succeed in securing eternal glory, and stand as saviors, and as kings and priests to our God, we will save our posterity."[18]

Parents who have kept their covenants and done their best need not despair when a child wanders. They have not failed. President David O. McKay once counseled that "no other success can compensate for failure in the home."[19] Elder John K. Carmack reassured the parents of struggling children that they should not misapply this principle and assume that their presumed failure has outweighed all their best efforts: "Because this statement was intended to inspire parents to become or stay involved with their children, it should not be taken to mean that parents who have indeed put great time, effort, and sacrifice into parenting, and yet who have still not reaped the desired rewards, have failed."[20]

It's important to note that parents are not entirely responsible for the personalities of their children. Each child of God is unique. After carefully reiterating that parents have the greatest responsibility and influence in the development of a child, President Howard W. Hunter taught, "Parents' hearts are ofttimes broken, yet they must realize that the ultimate responsibility lies with the child after parents have taught correct principles. . . . Perhaps there are children who have come into the world that would challenge any set of parents under any set of circumstances. Likewise, perhaps there are others who would bless the lives of, and be a joy to, almost any father or mother."[21] Heavenly Father is deserving of our trust in Him; He knows our hearts, and He knows our children. We must respect and understand the doctrine of agency, and believe in the enabling power of the Atonement to strengthen the parent and heal the child.

We mortal parents are not always patient, especially with ourselves. Sometimes we quickly misjudge whether we have succeeded or failed in our parenting, but both we and our children are eternal beings. An eternal perspective on today's trials can give us the proper focus.

"There is much which lieth in futurity," the Prophet Joseph Smith said. "Therefore . . . let us cheerfully do all things that lie in our power; and then may we stand still, with the utmost assurance, to see the salvation of God, and for his arm to be revealed."[22]

Because our mother hearts are so tied to our children, it is natural to hurt when they are hurting. But that pain can be swallowed up in the Atonement of Jesus Christ. In many cases, He is the only one who can make it better, but He lets us help. The hymn "Dear to the Heart of the Shepherd" testifies of the Savior's love for those who wander and invites us to be a part of His rescuing mission.

> *Green are the pastures inviting;*
> *Sweet are the waters and still.*
> *Lord, we will answer thee gladly,*
> *"Yes, blessed Master, we will!*
> *Make us thy true undershepherds;*
> *Give us a love that is deep.*
> *Send us out into the desert,*
> *Seeking thy wandering sheep."*[23]

I love the word *undershepherd*. It reflects the true nature of our parenting. We are apprentices to the Good Shepherd. We participate in His work and learn His craft, and He offers His help in caring for our lambs. "He shall feed his flock like a shepherd: he shall gather the lambs with his arm, and carry them in his bosom, and shall gently lead those that are with young."[24] He promises to gently lead parents. As we love and pray and keep covenants, we become like He is and participate in His work of saving souls. In so many ways, this is our true motherhood mission: to make His work our work so that we will know Him well.

CHAPTER 10

## *Grace and the Covenant*

MOTHERHOOD IS AN OVERWHELMING RESPONSIBILITY. Jesus Christ has shown us a flawless example of nurturing a child, but there are some days that, despite my best efforts, I simply know I am not the mother I need to be. Exhaustion, discouragement, opposition, or simple irritation get in the way. Will my children turn out okay in spite of me? Will I ever become the mother I believe I should be? How can I possibly meet everyone's needs when I consistently disappoint even myself?

If there is one reassurance I would hope to instill in covenant mothers everywhere, it is this: you are doing better than you think you are, and the Savior recognizes your efforts. When Jesus Christ praised His disciples for serving Him and feeding Him and visiting Him, they had no recollection of doing those things for Him. They didn't think they had served Him, but Jesus reassured, "Inasmuch as ye have done it unto one of the least of these my brethren, ye have done it unto me."[1] Service toward your children counts as service to Him. Jesus Christ asks for our best efforts, understands our circumstances and our hearts, and offers His grace.

It is not easy to see the joy or even the progress we have made when we feel like we are failing. I remember one difficult Sunday in particular. I don't think my day would have been any different if I had taken three pet monkeys to church instead of my own children. That children's song "Reverently, Quietly"[2] was not inspired by my children—maybe *for* my children but not *by* them.

After exchanging half annoyed, half shocked eye rolls with my husband several times across the pew, I was beginning to feel discouraged. I consciously had to rein in my anger so I could take the sacrament and not feel blasphemous about it. I was overwhelmed by my children. I had obviously failed to teach them correct behavior, or at least had failed to wrestle them into submission. Sundays can occasionally feel overwhelming anyway, because in addition to my own offspring, I often have other church responsibilities in which I feel equally inadequate. So in one of those near-to-tears moments, I heard the last speaker say amen, and we began to sing the closing hymn. I quote two of the four verses:

> *Shrink not from your duty, however unpleasant,*
> *But follow the Savior, your pattern and friend.*
> *Our little afflictions, tho painful at present,*
> *Ere long, with the righteous, in glory will end.*
> *Be fixed in your purpose, for Satan will try you;*
> *The weight of your calling he perfectly knows.*
> *Your path may be thorny, but Jesus is nigh you;*
> *His arm is sufficient, tho demons oppose.* [3]

I won't go into what my interpretation of *demons* was at that moment, but it's sufficient to say that the hymn became a poignant, personal message from my Heavenly Father. I literally felt His tangible encouragement and sensed that my shame was unnecessary. I felt His love, and I knew I was not alone. If it's true for me, it must be true for all moms. He recognizes our efforts and honors them, and He understands how we feel. His sufficient arm will reach out after us. He is truly nigh.

Elder Jeffrey R. Holland pleaded with parents to draw upon the Lord's help in raising our children: "We are not alone, and we do not tremble as if abandoned. In doing our part, we can live the gospel and defend its principles. We can declare to others the sure Way, the saving Truth, the joyful Life. We can personally repent in any way we need to repent, and when we have done all, we can pray. In all these ways we can bless one another and especially those who need our protection the most—the children. As parents we can hold life together the way it is always held together—with love and faith, passed on to the next generation, one child at a time."[4]

I can't help but think of the times Jesus made people's meager offerings be just enough because of their faith. When He fed the five thousand, He didn't whip up a meal out of thin air, though He certainly could have. Instead, He gathered what the people had, and then He added to it. He made it be enough. Jesus had His disciples gather the food and then distribute it. He could have done it all Himself, but He gave others opportunities to serve. Parenting is not a system of efficiency. I'm sure He could parent my children much better than I can, but He allows me to do it because I learn how to be more like Him in the process. And even in all of my inefficiency, He helps me do His work.

When He and His disciples observed people bringing their offerings to the treasury at the temple, He praised the poor widow woman even though she only gave two tiny mites—a seemingly insignificant offering compared to what everyone else offered. "She of her want did cast in *all that she had.*"[5] Once again, the Savior showed us His attitude toward what we are able to give. He does not demand a flawless offering, and He honors and appreciates our best efforts. He calls them enough.

The Bible Dictionary defines grace as "divine means of help or strength, given through the bounteous mercy and love of Jesus Christ" and adds that "this grace is an enabling power that allows men and women to lay hold on eternal life and exaltation after they have expended their own best efforts." Will our best efforts be perfect? No, because we are not perfect, and our Heavenly Father does not expect perfection that is not made complete through Jesus Christ. Only through Him can our ultimate perfection even be an option.

President Uchtdorf pleaded with the women of the Church to be gentler with themselves and rely more on our Savior: "May I invite you to rise to the great potential within you. But don't reach beyond your capacity. Don't set goals beyond your capacity to achieve. Don't feel guilty or dwell on thoughts of failure. Don't compare yourself with others. Do the best you can, and the Lord will provide the rest. Have faith and confidence in Him, and you will see miracles happen in your life and the lives of your loved ones."[6] When I read that charge from an apostle of God, I feel a huge sense of relief and freedom to be exactly who I am. A *me* kind of mom. I am not competing with any other mother out there, and there are some really great ones. I can look to righteous women as examples and improve realistically in any way I know how, but if I do it all with the Lord's help and with my eye on *His* approval, I can feel at peace.

What about mothers who struggle with situations that literally stretch them further than they believe they are capable of being stretched? Maybe you have a child who has enrolled you in Parenting 505,[7] or maybe you are parenting alone.[8] Does the principle of grace apply to you too? Not only does grace extend itself to the deepest struggles of the heart, but I also believe it is offered *especially* for difficult circumstances.

President Hinckley told the story of a single mother who reached a breaking point of exhaustion and frustration with her five children. One night as she stood outside her house and stared at the lighted windows and heard the noisy bustle of her kids, she half jokingly asked Heavenly Father to take her back home to Him instead. The Spirit quickly gave her this reply: "No, little one, you can't come to me now. . . . But I can come to you."[9] This is the healing balm of grace. He will come to us.

President Boyd K. Packer testified, "All too often, a parent is left alone to raise children. The Lord has a way of strengthening that parent to meet alone what should be the responsibility of two parents."[10] In other words, no parent truly parents alone.

In one of my favorite talks on motherhood, "Because She Is a Mother," Elder Jeffrey R. Holland reassures mothers everywhere that they can rely on heaven for the support they need in their monumental responsibilities. It is a talk worth hours of study and thought, but consider this small excerpt of reassurance:

> May I say to mothers collectively, in the name of the Lord, you are magnificent. You are doing terrifically well. The very fact that you have been given such a responsibility is everlasting evidence of the trust your Father in Heaven has in you. He knows that your giving birth to a child does not immediately propel you into the circle of the omniscient. If you and your husband will strive to love God and live the gospel yourselves; if you will plead for that guidance and comfort of the Holy Spirit promised to the faithful; if you will go to the temple to both make and claim the promises of the most sacred covenants a woman or man can make in this world; if you will show others, including your children, the same caring, compassionate, forgiving heart you want heaven to show you; if you try your best to be the best parent you can be, you will have done all that a human being can do and all that God expects you to do.[11]

This is a lesson we must learn over and over again. Discouraging days return often, and through messages from the scriptures, the Spirit, and our prophets and apostles, we begin to gain assurance of its truth.

I had a monumental meltdown once. A put-my-head-down-on-the-desk-and-cry kind of meltdown. I also cried in the kitchen and again in my bathroom and up and down some stairs and halls. I had no extraordinary reason; I had just reached what felt like the farthest corner of my limit, however pathetic it may have been. In retrospect, I like to call this entry in my motherhood story "The Parable of the Ranch Dressing." Let me explain why.

I went to bed too late, and my children woke up too early. I lay in bed listening to them crack each other up with jokes you have to be in kindergarten to appreciate. Grant came to my bedside to tattle that Clark was playing the game downstairs that they'd been grounded from yesterday. I sent him back to deliver a warning, and a few minutes later, I could hear them both playing that same game. I heard (and felt) bumping, laughing, wrestling, and fighting.

I finally progressed to breakfast and scavenged around in the kitchen because I was completely out of groceries. The noise, scuffling, and lame jokes continued. I tried in vain to hush the boys so they wouldn't wake up Natalie. They did, of course. It was one of those mornings where I dreaded getting out of bed and starting the day. (This happens occasionally when the day seems out of control before I'm even awake enough to face it. It usually fades once I get up and start moving. This time, it didn't.)

I found dishes in the sink and cottage cheese on the floor, table, wall, and door. Grant couldn't find his library book. "Hurry!" I bellowed down the hall. "You're going to miss the bus, and I'm not taking you." It was cold outside, and I was in a constant state of chill, even in my house. If I had to leave, I desperately needed to go to the store and to the post office (dread, dread, dreaded task) to mail Christmas cards and a package that I'd been meaning to send for at least a week.

"Matt, is the printer working yet?" I asked. "I need to print the address labels for my cards." He had been studying for finals and couldn't get it to work ever since the Internet had gone down the week before. On his way out the door, he handed me a network code on a Post-it note and claimed it would be easy for me to punch it in somewhere and make the computer recognize our printer. I was bathing Natalie and told him to put it on the desk.

As I walked downstairs, I passed the waist-high reminder of laundry that needed to be done. Sigh. *Oh, great, look what the boys did to the playroom this morning. Where's that blasted Post-it note?* It wasn't on the desk. I called Matt and finally found it on my bed.

I tried, tried, tried to get the printer to work but found myself beyond frustration. I called Matt again, and he couldn't really help me over the phone. In a highly irritated state of mind, I tried a few more things and somehow managed to disconnect the Internet all together. *Noooooo!* I tried again to fix it, but no luck. No Internet. No printer. No labels. No Christmas cards. The sour self-talk continued. *Too late; it will never get mailed on time. I spent too much money on them. No Internet? Now I can't even transfer money to my account to go grocery shopping. That's it.*

I hit a wall, dropped my head on the desk, and cried. Pretty hard. Clark wanted to ask me some questions, and I answered the best I could, but I wanted to get away.

The phone rang, and I composed myself. It was my neighbor, and she wanted to borrow some ranch dressing for her boys' lunch. A wave of frustration set over me because I remembered I had *no groceries*. I told her I didn't know if I had anything, but I'd check. She assured me it was fine if I didn't. I opened the fridge and found some. I told her I had less than a quarter bottle, and it wasn't even regular, traditional ranch. It was the three-cheese kind. I sort of apologized that I didn't have more or the right kind, and she said it sounded just fine. We agreed that Clark would drop it off on his way to the kindergarten bus stop.

Matt called back and asked about the printer. I started to cry again, and he (wisely) decided he'd just call back a little later and promised he'd help when he got home. I managed to keep my tears to a minimum while I fed Clark and Natalie a piecemeal lunch and got Clark out the door for school. I put Natalie in her room for quiet time, and the floodgates opened again.

There was no place to hide. Every room had some glaring pile or reminder of something else I needed to clean or do or wrap or fix or fold or put away. More tears. I thought about my grandma who had a nervous breakdown once, but she had nine children and lived in an old drafty home and had no money to buy groceries. My life was so much easier than hers. *What is wrong with me?* All my thoughts started with, "*I can't . . . I can't . . . I can't . . . I just can't.*"

I was on the verge of coming completely undone. I stood at my bedroom window and stared out across the street. I saw into my neighbor's house, where she was feeding her children lunch at the table. With my ranch dressing.

Unexpectedly, this is what my brain said to me: *You know, Stephanie, maybe you're like that ranch dressing. It didn't seem like enough, and it wasn't the "traditional" kind, and you assumed it wasn't what was wanted or needed. But it was.* I looked at my neighbor's happy little lunch scene. *It accomplished exactly what it was needed for, and everything's fine. It was enough.*

I took a deep breath and thought, *What does Satan want me to do right now?* (It seemed a little more concrete at the moment than *What would Jesus do?*) He probably wanted me to crawl into bed and never get out. I did get in bed, but I said a prayer. I told Heavenly Father I couldn't do this on my own—even stupid laundry and wiping cottage cheese off the door. I needed help outside of myself to get this stuff done. I sat up, and the first thought that came to my mind was, *Start with the red coat.*

I looked at the coat I'd left on the floor by my closet for a minute and felt grateful that God had given me a place to start, because I felt too overwhelmed by the amount of stuff I needed to do. And little by little, I made progress. When the kids got home from school, I had some warm banana chocolate-chip muffins waiting for them and a long list of chores and three dice. They rolled dice and did the chores with the matching numbers. We all worked together for a couple of hours and got a lot done. I felt lighter and lighter, and by the end of the day, I was myself again. I felt silly about my meltdown. It's only happened two or three times since I got married more than a full decade ago, but it has happened. And it might again—but God helps me crawl out when I finally break down enough to admit how much I need Him.

I don't think I'll ever see a bottle of ranch dressing again without remembering that no matter how little I have to offer or how different I feel from what I think I should be, I am enough (with God's help) to accomplish anything that really needs to be done. Like the woman with an issue of blood who reached out in desperation toward the Savior, I found His attention and His reassurance. "Daughter, be of good comfort; thy faith hath made thee whole."[12]

We are mothers. We are enough. We are everything our children need in order to become all they are meant to be . . . with His help. However we fall short, He will make up the difference. He has given us His children because He *trusts* us to rely upon Him for their care. Our covenant relationship with Him sets up a contract where, despite our failures, Jesus Christ will make us whole if we seek His help and forgiveness. This covenant does not exclude motherhood. When, like Hannah of old, we promise to raise our children up unto the Lord, He accepts our offering and does His part to help us fulfill our promises. I believe that help can even come by angels, whether living or beyond the veil. He meets our needs. By the grace of God, we become the mothers He wants us to be. We participate in His work and His glory, and both we and our children are blessed.

CHAPTER 11

## The Eternal Influence of Covenant Motherhood

By making and keeping covenants, we participate in the amazing opportunity to secure for ourselves and our posterity blessings for all eternity. The Atonement of Jesus Christ makes it possible for us to qualify for those blessings even when we sometimes fall short of our promised discipleship. As we strive to keep those promises, our choices have the potential for eternal influence.

Sister Julie B. Beck taught on many occasions that "mothers who know" make an important difference because "there is eternal influence and power in motherhood."[1] Elder Bednar testified that our small, seemingly insignificant acts of discipleship are like tiny brushstrokes that, over time, create a beautiful and meaningful masterpiece.[2] And prophets all the way back before the coming of the Messiah have declared that "by small and simple things are great things brought to pass."[3]

As we go through the daily details of our mothering, the small things are more meaningful than we recognize. Like signs and tokens of our covenant relationship with Christ, the simple emulation of His attributes binds us to Him and makes us like Him. Piece by piece, we build a life and a home and a family based on the doctrines of Jesus Christ; we create in slow motion.

So often I am tempted to discount the impact of the things that take up most of my time—the logistical duties like cooking, bathing, and laundering. Maybe Alma could read my mind and was speaking directly to me when he said, "Now ye may suppose that this is foolishness in me; but behold . . . the Lord God doth work by means to bring about his great and eternal purposes; and by very small means the Lord doth confound the wise and bringeth about the salvation of many souls."[4] I continue to learn that Heavenly Father sees things as they really are, and I often do not. Philosopher Thomas Moore claimed, "The ordinary acts we practice every day at home are of more importance to the soul than their simplicity might suggest."[5] In response to our longing to sometimes do things that are more "spectacular," Mother Teresa gently reminds, "We can do no great things—only small things with great love."[6]

Importance manifests itself as the powerful influence a mother can have in the life and the mind of a child and future generations. A mother's testimony and a mother's example can remain with a child as a candle to light the way in times of darkness. I hope my children will better understand the Savior's ability to love and help them because they have felt and understood *my* sincere love. I will have succeeded as a mother if my faith and testimony bolster their faith when it needs kindling.

Stories from the Book of Mormon show us many examples of children—both stalwart and wayward—whose lives were profoundly influenced by the teachings and guidance of righteous parents. Nephi, Sam, Jacob, and Joseph maintained faith in the Lord and received answers to prayers even in times of great uncertainty because of lessons they learned from their father, Lehi. Enos wrestled before the Lord in prayer and found forgiveness for his sins and promised blessings for his brethren because he drew upon the principles he had often heard his father teach.

Alma the Younger literally turned his life from sin to exuberant discipleship through his conversion—a conversion modeled by and desperately prayed for by at least one faithful parent. The stripling warriors faced battle with courage because of their profound faith in the truths and testimonies passed on by their mothers. Guided by his father's example and conviction, Moroni was able to carry on diligently with his mission despite opposition at every turn and no other human support.

These stories serve as an inspiration to all of us who read the Book of Mormon. The legacy of righteous parents long ago now serves as a fount of testimony for disciples of Jesus Christ throughout the world. Even if my simple acts of mothering are not recorded or distributed in books of scripture, they can leave a lasting influence "to all generations and for eternity."[7]

Sister Julie B. Beck assured, "When mothers know who they are and who God is and have made covenants with Him, they will have great power and influence for good on their children."[8]

For the sake of analysis, let's juxtapose some questions that address common confusion in the modern world about the role of mothers—even among LDS women—with answers from the counsel of modern-day prophets and apostles.

*Many women are educated, talented, and extremely capable. Isn't it a waste of their skills to spend time with children when they could make a bigger difference in the public sphere? When so many options are available, doesn't it make sense to outsource the more menial tasks of childcare so that women can do bigger things?*

President Spencer W. Kimball: "No matter what you read or hear, no matter what the differences of circumstances you observe in the lives of women about you, it is important for you Latter-day Saint women to understand that the Lord holds motherhood and mothers sacred and in the highest esteem. He has entrusted to His daughters the great responsibility of bearing and nurturing children.

This is the great, irreplaceable work of women. . . . Mothers have a sacred role. They are partners with God, as well as with their own husbands, first in giving birth to the Lord's spirit children and then in rearing those children so they will serve the Lord and keep his commandments."[9]

*No one seems to notice the work I do, which makes it feel like it doesn't matter. I wonder if there would be more rewards or recognition in other pursuits.*

President Ezra Taft Benson: "No accomplishment transcends the building of the character of a son or a daughter of God."[10]

*This is a world with so much access to information. There are schools and organizations and extracurricular activities that can teach our children and help develop their character. Is a mother's influence really that important?*

Elder M. Russell Ballard: "There is nothing in this world as personal, as nurturing, or as life changing as the influence of a righteous woman."[11]

*Sometimes, even within the gospel, it feels like mothers with young children aren't able to accomplish all that they are supposed to do. When my children are so young and needy, how can I possibly do family history work, be a missionary, attend the temple regularly, and be an active contributor to the missions of the Church?*

Elder Robert D. Hales: "The greatest missionary work we will ever do will be in our homes. . . .

The greatest family history work that we will do will be within our own homes. . . .

The greatest rescue, the greatest activation will be in our homes. . . .

The greatest faith we have will be within our homes as we remain strong in the trials and tribulations of parenthood. . . .

The greatest love and the greatest teachings should be in our homes."[12]

*I try so hard to do what's right and to be a good mom, but it's so difficult to measure any success. My children don't seem to make much progress with all of the things I'm trying to teach them, and I often feel weary. Am I really making an important difference in their lives?*

Elder Richard G. Scott: "Who can justly measure the righteous influence of a mother's love? What enduring fruits result from the seeds of truth that a mother carefully plants and lovingly cultivates in the fertile soil of a child's trusting mind and heart? As a mother you have been given divine instincts to help you sense your child's special talents and unique capacities. With your husband you can nurture, strengthen, and cause those traits to flower."[13]

*Some people seem to leave their mark on history in big ways, and my contribution is so small and unrecognizable. Does Heavenly Father really value what I'm doing, and does it add value to our society?*

Elder Neal A. Maxwell: "When the real history of mankind is fully disclosed, will it feature the echoes of gunfire or the shaping sound of lullabies? The great armistices made by military men or the peacemaking of women in homes and in neighborhoods? Will what happened in cradles and kitchens prove to be more controlling than what happened in congresses? When the surf of the centuries has made the great pyramids so much sand, the everlasting family will still be standing, because it is a celestial institution, formed outside telestial time. The women of God know this."[14]

In the day-to-day minutiae of our mothering responsibilities, it is so easy to lose sight of the eternal reach of our efforts. Our Heavenly Father always sees and recognizes our power for good, and so does Satan. This is why marriages and families are under attack; living prophets and apostles have warned that "the disintegration of the family will bring upon individuals, communities, and nations the calamities foretold by ancient and modern prophets."[15] Sister Sheri Dew explained, "Satan has declared war on motherhood. He knows that those who rock the cradle can rock his earthly empire. And he knows that without righteous mothers loving and leading the next generation, the kingdom of God will fail."[16]

Covenant mothers, we must not fail. We must believe and embrace the power within us to make a difference in this world and in the next—one child, one family, and one community at a time. As we unite in an effort to be examples of the mission of Jesus Christ, we are individually and collectively blessed with His grace. With His help, we accomplish more than we realize.

It may appear that there are not many stories about women in the scriptures, but there are actually almost six hundred women mentioned in our canon of scripture.[17] Their stories are not always long, but they offer great insight into the powerful influence of their righteousness across generations, and no generation exists or prospers without a patriarch *and* a matriarch. There are three women from the scriptures and Church history who have been stand-out examples to me of what God can do with simple, humble women. Abish, Lucy Mack Smith, and Mary saw themselves as ordinary, but each lived with integrity according to the knowledge she had. As you consider each woman's story, notice the magnificent scope of her influence.

In Alma chapter 19, we read the story of Abish, a Lamanite woman. When Ammon preached the gospel of Jesus Christ to the Lamanite king Lamoni, the king was overcome and fell to the ground. He later arose and shared his joy with his wife, and they both "[sank] down, being overpowered by the Spirit." Ammon was also overcome, and all three of them lay upon the ground. This Spirit-induced unconsciousness did not end there; except for Abish, the servants of the king who had witnessed it were also filled with fear and the power of God, and eventually the whole household collapsed. This was quite a scene, and Abish knew it was an opportunity. She herself was a believer because of a remarkable vision her father had once had. The influence of a parent prepared her to recognize the power of God when it was manifest, and she wanted to make it known to her fellow Lamanites. The scriptures give the following account: "She knew that it was the power of God; and supposing that this opportunity, by making known unto the people what had happened among them, that by beholding this scene it would cause them to believe in the power of God, therefore she ran forth from house to house, making it known unto the people."[18]

Soon a crowd had gathered around this extraordinary scene, and their curiosity and awe began to turn to skepticism. They wondered aloud about the cause, and one man drew his sword to kill Ammon, but he immediately fell dead. The crowd became even more agitated and debated what kind of role the Great Spirit had played in this apparent tragedy. As contention grew, Abish became sorrowful, and she stepped forward and "took the queen by the hand, that perhaps she might raise her from the ground."[19] The queen did arise, lifted the King also, and together they bore powerful testimony to the crowd about the merits and mercy of Jesus Christ. "And as many as heard [their] words believed, and were converted unto the Lord."[20]

Abish was one woman. She did not have a calling, nor had she ever previously made known her testimony, but when she took the initiative to share her conviction with others, the result was remarkable. An entire crowd of hardened Lamanites heard and received the gospel through her actions. They eventually became the people known as the Ammonites, who made covenants with the Lord and were filled with His Spirit. Among the crowd that day would have been the women who later raised the stripling warriors. We often pay tribute to these women for their powerful influence on young "men who were true at all times in whatsoever thing they were entrusted. Yea, they were men of truth and soberness, for they had been taught to keep the commandments of God and to walk uprightly before him."[21] Their tribute is well deserved, and they provide an excellent model for all mothers, but it might not have been possible were it not for Abish's courage. One righteous woman can change the course of generations.

The Prophet of the Restoration of the gospel of Jesus Christ was Joseph Smith. His mother was Lucy Mack Smith. As a modern-day mother, I cannot even begin to imagine the challenges of a homesteading mother in the 1800s. Her day was full of manual labor and the care of a husband and many children. Sickness was frequent and debilitating and frightening. Family economy was precarious, and it was often a struggle to provide even the staples of life. I wonder how much stress and fatigue were a part of her daily life. If she was anything like I am, I can guess that she felt utterly overwhelmed many days.

I studied her history written in her own words and learned that the struggle to find answers to her own religious questions sometimes became a point of contention with her husband. As I read, I was struck by one powerful detail: she wrote, "I retired to a grove not far distant, where I prayed to the Lord in behalf of my husband—that the true gospel might be presented to him, and that his heart might be softened so as to receive it."[22] I wonder how many times Lucy sought solace among the trees. My heart tells me that it must have been a habit for her to remove herself from the burdens she felt and seek out the Lord's guidance. It is only speculation, but perhaps she went there frequently for answers and strength and direction in facing the challenges of her day-to-day responsibilities and the trials that so often presented themselves.

Whatever the case may be, it is not surprising that her son Joseph, when faced with his own religious dilemma, retired to a grove of trees and offered up perhaps the most significant prayer in the history of mankind. Where did he learn to seek out answers to his questions? Where did he witness a model of kneeling in prayer? How did he know that he might find God among the nearby trees? Is it possible that a mother's example of beseeching the Lord in times of uncertainty paved the way for a fourteen-year-old boy to be called of God to restore the gospel of Jesus Christ upon the earth? Absolutely. The same prayer she offered in a grove of trees was *answered*. The answer came to her young son, with his own personal longing, who repeated in another grove of trees the essence of her original prayer! Lucy Mack Smith's story teaches me that notwithstanding any despair or inadequacy I might feel, I can set an example for my children, even in one thing, that could change the course of history. It is an amazing prospect.

Later in Joseph's life, when he and Hyrum were afflicted with cholera in the Missouri wilderness, they were sure they were near death. Just at the point when they thought they could live no longer, Hyrum leapt up and told Joseph that he had a vision of their mother praying for them beneath an apple tree, pleading with the Lord to protect them and spare their lives. He then declared, "The Spirit testifies, that her prayers, united with ours, will be answered." Consider the power in Joseph's reply: "Oh, my mother! How often have your prayers been the means of assisting us when the shadows of death encompassed us."[23] One righteous mother can draw upon the power of God and bless her family in ways that influence generations and dispensations.

Finally, in the New Testament, we find the story of Mary, the mother of Jesus. What a wonderful example she is to me of righteous motherhood. We know that she was young, she was a virgin, and she was espoused to be married to Joseph. We don't know if she had experienced any previous contact with angels, but she was certainly astonished when Gabriel announced to her that she had been chosen as the vessel to bear God's own Son. Mary considered herself to be an ordinary woman, and upon hearing this news, she must have been flooded with self-doubt and inadequacy. In fact, when the angel first greeted her and told her that she was highly favored of the Lord and blessed among women, "she was troubled at his saying, and cast in her mind what manner of salutation this should be." Even when he reassured her and explained the nature of his visit and her calling, she replied, "How shall this be . . . ?"[24]

I wonder at her feelings at that moment. Gabriel testified that with God, nothing is impossible, but she must have felt a whirlwind of doubt and fear and overwhelming bewilderment. Her response has always amazed me with its humility and powerful surrender: "Behold the handmaid of the Lord; be it unto me according to thy word."[25] Her answer echoed the preexisting words of the Son she was yet to bear: "Here am I, send me."[26]

One Sunday, many years ago, I taught a Sunday School lesson about the ultimate sacrifice that Jesus paid as He atoned for all mankind in the Garden of Gethsemane. We discussed His suffering, and I paused as I pondered His heartbreaking plea, "Father, if thou be willing, remove this cup from me: nevertheless *not my will, but thine, be done.*"[27] My mind reflected on Mary's response to the angel, and it dawned on me that this principle of surrendering to God's will was something Jesus had probably learned *from His mother*. She had given Him an example of courage to do what Heavenly Father required even when the prospective challenges were almost incomprehensible. It seems that Jesus' mother possessed the same category of faith that He would need in order to perform the most important act in human history.

The scriptures testify that as a boy, Jesus "increased in wisdom and stature, and in favour with God and man."[28] While He was naturally endowed with many of these attributes, we cannot underestimate the influence Mary must have had in the development of His character. After all, she had been chosen as His mother because of her own favor with God. Her loving watchcare over Jesus was returned to her as her Son languished on the cross; despite the literal weight of the world, He pleaded with John to care for His mother.

Abish, Lucy Mack Smith, and Mary are covenant mothers because they lived their faith in a way that profoundly affected generations. We too can have powerful influence even if we do not convert a nation, raise a prophet, or train up God's Only Begotten Son. Sister Elaine S. Dalton has declared on several occasions, "Can one righteous young woman change the world? The answer is a resounding 'yes!' You have the Holy Ghost as your guide, and He 'will show . . . you all things . . . [you] should do' (2 Nephi 32:5). It is the daily consistent things you do that will strengthen you to be a leader and an example—daily prayer, daily scripture study, daily obedience, daily service to others. As you do these things, you will grow closer to the Savior and become more and more like Him."[29]

A few days before I sat down to write this chapter, I attended the funeral of my mom's best friend. I felt the Holy Ghost's influence as I saw the large room full of people who had been touched by her obedient life and loving service. Her seven children stood and bore testimony of the influence of her Christlike attributes in their lives—the very same attributes we have explored in the chapters of this book. One daughter said, "Everything I am and everything I hope to become, I owe to the bright light of my mother's testimony." To quote Sister Julie B. Beck, "*That* is influence. *That* is power."[30]

As literal daughters of God, all women have inherited a portion of His divinity and His power. On a smaller scale, especially when armed with covenants, we are endowed with the power to do within our families and communities the work that God Himself does throughout His universe. We bless souls and turn them to Christ and toward our heavenly home. As the chapters of this book have outlined, motherhood is a reflection of the same roles Jesus Christ played out in His ministry and service to all mankind.

Just as the Messiah's covenant relationship with us is binding throughout eternity, so is our covenant relationship with our children. President Joseph F. Smith taught:

> [Mothers], you do not know how far your influence extends. A mother that is successful in raising a good boy, or girl, to imitate her example and to follow her precepts through life, sows the seeds of virtue, honor and integrity and of righteousness in their hearts that will be felt through all their career in life; and wherever that boy or girl goes, as man or woman, in whatever society they mingle, the good effects of the example of that mother upon them will be felt; and it will never die, because it will extend from them to their children from generation to generation.[31]

Motherhood is a monumental investment, and sometimes our offerings don't make sense in the moment. When Adam and Eve left the Garden of Eden and began their mortal life as parents, they made sacrifices and offerings to the Lord. They did so to be obedient, but they didn't really understand *why*. The angel taught Adam that those sacrifices were "a similitude of the sacrifice of the Only Begotten of the Father, which is full of grace and truth."[32] So it is with motherhood. Much of what we do as mothers is an offering to our families and to Heavenly Father because, like Adam and Eve, we love them and we want to be obedient. Repeated offerings require sacrifices—big and small, some daily, some deep. All of these offerings are symbols of our Savior and are meant to point us to Him.

What about our sleepless nights, frenzied meal planning, never-ending laundry or housework, hugging, wiping, hurrying, and worrying? Is it all too small to count? No. It is not mundane to Heavenly Father. It is our offering, and it is *all* sacred.

I am not a perfect mother, but I know my role as a mother is divine. Everything I do for my children is designed to bring me closer to my Savior and to bring my children along with me. This process of emulating His mission in all the particularities of *my* mission helps me be perfected in Him and by Him. It helps me know Christ better because I am learning to be like Him. I know that Heavenly Father loves me and trusts me and helps me be the mother He knows I can be. For that opportunity and its accompanying grace, my gratitude is as eternal as my influence. Covenant motherhood is my destiny, His work, our glory, and eternity's joy.

# Endnotes

## Introduction

1. Heber J. Grant, J. Reuben Clark, and David O. McKay, in James R. Clark, comp. *Messages of the First Presidency of The Church of Jesus Christ of Latter-day Saints*, vol. 6, *1935–1951* (Salt Lake City: Bookcraft, 1975), 178.

2. Boyd K. Packer, "For Time and All Eternity," *Ensign*, November 1993.

3. Neal A. Maxwell, *Not My Will, But Thine* (Salt Lake City: Bookcraft, 1988), 53–54.

4. Jacob 4:13.

5. Neal A. Maxwell. *". . . A More Excellent Way"* (Salt Lake City: Deseret Book, 1967), 84–85.

6. 1 Samuel 1:11.

7. "The Lord's Covenant People," in *Gospel Principles* (Salt Lake City: The Church of Jesus Christ of Latter-day Saints, 2009), 81.

8. Dallin H. Oaks, "Have You Been Saved?" *Ensign*, May 1998.

9. Julie B. Beck, "A 'Mother Heart'," *Ensign*, May 2004.

10. Susan W. Tanner, "Strengthening Future Mothers," *Liahona*, June 2005.

11. Ezra Taft Benson, "Jesus Christ—Gifts and Expectations," *Ensign*, December 1988.

# Chapter 1

1. Moses 1:33.

2. Genesis 1:31.

3. M. Russell Ballard, "Great Shall Be the Peace of Thy Children," *Ensign*, April 1994.

4. Sheri L. Dew, "Are We Not All Mothers?" *Ensign*, November 2001.

5. Genesis 1:26.

6. Moses 1:39.

7. "Chapter 14: Preparing for an Eternal Marriage and Family," *Teachings of Presidents of the Church: David O. McKay* (Salt Lake City: The Church of Jesus Christ of Latter-day Saints, 2003), 135.

8. Dieter F. Uchtdorf, "Happiness, Your Heritage," *Ensign*, November 2008.

9. Richard G. Scott, "The Joy of Living the Great Plan of Happiness," *Ensign*, November 1996.

10. Spencer W. Kimball, "Privileges and Responsibilities of Sisters," *Ensign*, November 1978.

11. Ibid.

12. Dieter F. Uchtdorf, "Happiness, Your Heritage," *Ensign*, November 2008.

13. Mary Ellen Smoot, "We Are Creators," *Ensign*, May 2000.

14. Ibid.

15. David A. Bednar, "'Ye Are the Temple of God,'" *Ensign*, September 2001.

## Chapter 2

1. Neil L. Andersen, "Tell Me the Stories of Jesus," *Ensign*, May 2010.

2. "The Family: A Proclamation to the World." Gordon B. Hinckley. "Stand Strong Against the Wiles of the World," *Ensign*, November 1995.

3. Matthew 14:13–16.

4. Neil L. Andersen, "Tell Me the Stories of Jesus," *Ensign*, May 2010.

5. Julie B. Beck, "Nourishing and Protecting the Family," May 1, 2009 Women's Conference Transcript.

6. First Presidency letter, February 11, 1999; in *Church News*, February 27, 1999, 3.

7. Doctrine and Covenants 64:33.

8. David A. Bednar, "More Diligent and Concerned at Home," *Ensign*, November 2009.

9. Corianton was Helaman's son and was rebuked for following after the harlot Isabel. The account of his father's response to his poor behavior can be found in Alma 39.

10. Neil L. Andersen, "Tell Me the Stories of Jesus," *Ensign*, May 2010.

11. Ibid.

12. Robert D. Hales, "Strengthening Families: Our Sacred Duty," *Ensign*, May 1999.

13. M. Russell Ballard, "Great Shall Be the Peace of Thy Children," *Ensign*, April 1994.

14. Gordon B. Hinckley, "Your Greatest Challenge, Mother," *Ensign*, November 2000.

15. Julie B. Beck, "Mothers Who Know," *Ensign*, November 2007.

16. Jeffrey R. Holland, "A Prayer for the Children," *Ensign*, May 2003.

17. John 1:37.

18. Spencer W. Kimball, "The Blessings and Responsibilities of Womanhood," *Ensign*, March 1976.

## Chapter 3

1. Dallin H. Oaks, "He Heals the Heavy Laden," *Ensign*, November 2006.

2. Jeffrey R. Holland, "Come Unto Me," *Ensign*, April 1998.

3. Matthew 9:20–22.

4. Matthew 8:2–4.

5. Matthew 9:36.

6. Sheri L. Dew, "Are We Not All Mothers?" *Ensign*, November 2001.

7. Ann Gerhart, "Laura Bush, Comforter In Chief; First Lady Works to Soothe a Shaken Nation," *The Washington Post*, September 19, 2001; C1.

8. John 16:33.

9. Gordon B. Hinckley, "Great Shall Be the Peace of Thy Children," *Ensign*, November 2000.

10. Jeffrey R. Holland, "Come Unto Me," *Ensign*, April 1998.

## Chapter 4

11. "The Family: A Proclamation to the World." Gordon B. Hinckley. "Stand Strong Against the Wiles of the World," *Ensign*, November 1995.

12. John 2:2–10.

13. Luke 5:6.

14. Matthew 17:27.

15. Mark 6:36–44.

16. Ibid.

17. Dieter F. Uchtdorf, "Providing in the Lord's Way," *Ensign*, November 2011.

18. J. Reuben Clark Jr., in *Conference Report*, April 1937, 22.

19. Proverbs 22:6.

20. *Cherished Experiences from the Writings of President David O. McKay*, comp. Clare Middlemiss (Salt Lake City: Deseret News Press,1955), 189.

21. John 21:9.

22. John 21:15–17.

23. Silvia H. Allred, "The Essence of Discipleship," *Ensign*, May 2011.

24. Camille Curtis Anderson, "The Fruit of Her Hands," *Ensign*, September 1996.

## Chapter 5

1. Luke 7:37–48.

2. Ibid.

3. John 9:11.

4. John 13:4–17.

5. 3 Nephi 31:12.

6. Genesis 9:12–15.

7. Russell M. Nelson, "Covenants," *Ensign*, November 2011.

8. Isaiah 1:18.

9. Revelation 1:5.

10. D. Todd Christofferson, "Born Again," *Ensign*, May 2008.

11. Clate W. Mask, Jr., "Standing Spotless Before the Lord," *Ensign*, May 2004.

12. Gregory A. Schwitzer, "Developing Good Judgment and Not Judging Others," *Ensign*, May 2010.

13. Chieko N. Okazaki, *Lighten Up!* (Salt Lake City: Deseret Book, 1993), 173–74.

14. Dallin H. Oaks, "What Think Ye of Christ?" *Ensign*, November 1988; emphasis added.

# Chapter 6

1. 3 Nephi 10:5.

2. Mark 11:15–17.

3. Matthew 18:6.

4. John 9:2–3.

5. John 8:3–11.

6. Julie B. Beck, "Nourishing and Protecting the Family," 2009 Women's Conference Transcripts.

7. Matthew 10:28.

8. Jeffrey R. Holland, "A Prayer for the Children," *Ensign*, May 2003.

9. Henry B. Eyring, "Finding Safety in Counsel," *Ensign*, May 1997.

10. Sheri L. Dew, "Are We Not All Mothers?" *Ensign*, November 2001.

11. Spencer W. Kimball, "Privileges and Responsibilities of Sisters," *Ensign*, November 1978.

12. Boyd K. Packer, "Do Not Fear," *Ensign*, May 2004.

13. "I have said lately that women are like lionesses at the gate of the home. Whatever happens in that home and family happens because she cares about it and it matters to her. She guards that gate, and things matter to that family if they matter to her." (Julie B. Beck, "Choose Ye This Day to Serve the Lord," address given April 29, 2010, BYU Women's Conference, 4.)

14. First Presidency letter, Feb. 11, 1999; cited in *Church News*, 27 February 1999, 3.

15. Virginia U. Jensen, "Creating Places of Security," *Ensign*, November 1997.

16. David A. Bednar, "Watching with All Perseverance," *Ensign*, May 2010.

# Chapter 7

1. John 17:21–23.

2. M. Russell Ballard, "Daughters of God," *Ensign*, May 2008.

3. John 13:34.

4. Isaiah 11:6.

5. 3 Nephi 17:23.

6. M. Russell Ballard, "Great Shall Be the Peace of Thy Children," *Ensign*, April 1994.

7. Moroni 7:47.

8. *Discourses of Brigham Young*, sel. John A. Widtsoe (Salt Lake City: Deseret Book, 1954), 271.

9. 1 John 4:8.

10. Spencer W. Kimball, "Privileges and Responsibilities of Sisters," *Ensign*, November 1978.

11. Julie B. Beck, "Mothers Who Know," *Ensign*, November 2007.

12. Psalm 23:4.

13. Isaiah 53:5.

14. 1 John 5:8.

15. Spencer W. Kimball, "Privileges and Responsibilities of Sisters," *Ensign*, November 1978.

16. Jeffrey R. Holland, "'Because She Is a Mother,'" *Ensign*, May 1997.

17. Matthew 10:39.

18. John 15:13.

19. See 3 Nephi 28:10.

# *Chapter 8*

1. Alma 7:11.

2. John 8:11.

3. Mark 2:5, 9.

4. Luke 7:47.

5. Matthew 18:21–22.

6. Matthew 5:36–44.

7. Matthew 7:1–5.

8. D&C 64:9–10.

9. Hebrews 12:2.

10. See Dieter F. Uchtdorf, "Happiness, Your Heritage," *Ensign*, November 2008.

11. Sheri L. Dew, "Are We Not All Mothers?" *Ensign*, November 2001.

12. Gordon B. Hinckley, "Your Greatest Challenge, Mother," *Ensign*, November 2000.

13. Matthew 11:29.

14. Mosiah 18:8–9.

15. Matthew 11:28; emphasis omitted.

16. 3 Nephi 22:10.

17. 2 Corinthians 12:7.

## Chapter 9

1. 2 Nephi 31:24.

2. See Obadiah 1:21.

3. John 6:39.

4. Luke 19:10.

5. Luke 15:24.

6. Their story is shared with permission, but the names have been changed.

7. Robert D. Hales, "Strengthening Families: Our Sacred Duty," *Ensign*, May 1999.

8. John K. Carmack, "When Our Children Go Astray," *Ensign*, February 1997.

9. James E. Faust, "Dear Are the Sheep That Have Wandered," *Ensign*, May 2003.

10. Robert D. Hales, "Our Duty to God: The Mission of Parents and Leaders to the Rising Generation," *Ensign*, May 2010.

11. Jeffrey R. Holland, "A Prayer for the Children," *Ensign*, May 2003.

12. Alma 34:18.

13. At the time this revelation was received, Emma Smith had lost one child and had been disowned by her father. She eventually lost six of her children to death.

14. Doctrine and Covenants 25:13.

15. Orson F. Whitney, *Conference Report*, April 1929, 110.

16. Brigham Young, in Joseph Fielding Smith, *Doctrines of Salvation*, comp. Bruce R. McConkie, 3 vols. (Salt Lake City: Bookcraft, 1955), 2:91.

17. Boyd K. Packer, "Our Moral Environment," *Ensign*, May 1992.

18. Lorenzo Snow, in *Collected Discourses*, comp. Brian H. Stuy, 5 vols. *1982–1993* (Burbank, CA: B.H.S., 1989), 3:364.

19. David O. McKay, *Conference Report*, April 1964, 5.

20. John K. Carmack. "When Our Children Go Astray," *Ensign*, February 1997.

21. Howard W. Hunter. "Parents' Concern for Children," *Ensign*, November 1983.

22. Doctrine & Covenants 123:15, 17.

23. "Dear to the Heart of the Shepherd," *Hymns*, no. 221.

24. Isaiah 40:11.

## Chapter 10

1. Matthew 25:40.

2. *Children's Songbook of The Church of Jesus Christ of Latter-day Saints* (Salt Lake City: The Church of Jesus Christ of Latter-day Saints, 1989) 26.

3. "The Time Is Far Spent," *Hymns*, no. 266.

4. Jeffrey R. Holland, "A Prayer for the Children," *Ensign*, May 2003.

5. Mark 12:44; emphasis added.

6. Dieter F. Uchtdorf, "The Influence of Righteous Women," *Liahona*, September 2009.

7. Lynn G. Robbins, "What Manner of Men and Women Ought Ye To Be?" *Ensign*, May 2011.

8. David S. Baxter, "Faith, Fortitude, Fulfillment: A Message to Single Parents," *Ensign*, May 2012.

9. Gordon B. Hinckley, "In the Arms of His Love," *Ensign*, November 2006.

10. Boyd K. Packer, "Children," *Ensign*, May 2002.

11. Jeffrey R. Holland, "'Because She Is a Mother,'" *Ensign*, May 1997.

12. Matthew 9:22.

# Chapter 11

1. Julie B. Beck, "Mothers Who Know," *Ensign*, November 2007.

2. David A. Bednar, "More Diligent and Concerned at Home," *Ensign*, November 2009.

3. Alma 37:6. See also two general conference talks by Elder M. Russell Ballard: "Finding Joy through Loving Service," *Ensign*, May 2011, and "Be Anxiously Engaged," *Ensign*, November 2012.

4. Ibid.

5. In Jack Canfield and Mark Victor Hansen, "On Parenting," *A 6th Bowl of Chicken Soup for the Soul*, http://books.google.com/books?id=cRHtDqPqe-YC&printsec=frontcover&dq=a+6th+bowl+of+chicken+soup+for+the+soul&hl=en&sa=X&ei=28a2UPGSFKXyigKOw4GwBg&ved=0CC0Q6AEwAA.

6. Mother Teresa, as quoted in *Life in the Spirit*, ed. Kathryn Spink (1983), 45.

7. D&C 109:24.

8. Julie B. Beck, "Mothers Who Know," *Ensign*, November 2007.

9. Spencer W. Kimball, "Privileges and Responsibilities of Sisters," *Ensign*, November 1978.

10. Ezra Taft Benson, "The Honored Place of Woman," *Ensign*, November 1981.

11. M. Russell Ballard, "Mothers and Daughters," *Ensign*, May 2010.

12. Robert D. Hales, "Our Duty to God: The Mission of Parents and Leaders to the Rising Generation," *Ensign*, May 2010.

13. Richard G. Scott, "The Eternal Blessings of Marriage," *Ensign*, May 2011.

14. Neal A. Maxwell, "The Women of God," *Ensign*, May 1978.

15. "The Family: A Proclamation to the World." Gordon B. Hinckley. "Stand Strong Against the Wiles of the World," *Ensign*, November 1995.

16. Sheri L. Dew, "Are We Not All Mothers?" *Ensign*, November 2001.

17. Heather Farrell, http://womeninthescriptures.blogspot.com/2011/03/setting-record-straight-there-really.html.

18. Alma 19:13, 17.

19. Alma 19: 29.

20. Alma 19:31.

21. Alma 53:20–21.

22. Lucy Mack Smith. *The History of Joseph Smith According to His Mother*, (American Fork, UT: Covenant Communications, 2000), 51.

23. Ibid., 215.

24. Luke 1:29, 34.

25. Luke 1:38.

26. Abraham 3:27.

27. Luke 22:42; emphasis added.

28. Luke 2:52.

29. Elaine S. Dalton, "It Shows in Your Face," *Ensign*, May 2006.

30. Julie B. Beck, "Mothers Who Know," *Ensign*, November 2007; emphasis added.

31. Joseph F. Smith, *Teachings of Presidents of the Church: Joseph F. Smith*, (Salt Lake City: The Church of Jesus Christ of Latter-day Saints, 1998), 30–38.

32. Moses 5:7.

# About the Author

STEPHANIE DIBB SORENSEN IS A mother to three children. She likes to consider them publicly charming and privately relentless. She and her husband, Matt, recently landed in Utah after spending the first decade of their marriage in the South and the Midwest. Their family enjoys camping together and taking road trips, and Stephanie loves to use all of their stories as case studies in studying, teaching, and writing about the gospel. After starting a blog several years ago, she discovered a passion for sharing real life mixed with real doctrine, and that planted a seed that grew into this book. She thinks motherhood is the hardest job in the world; therefore, it must be the most important. Second to mothering, Stephanie also teaches as an adjunct faculty member in the Department of Church History and Doctrine at BYU and teaches regularly at Especially for Youth. When she's not busy with her various projects, she loves napping, eating out, reading books, taking long walks, and other activities that make no noise.